"This readable and engaging *Handbook* clearly explains what Dual and Multiple Exceptionality (DME) is and then applies this understanding to teachers' daily classroom practice and its impact for learners. Written by experts in high learning potential and special educational needs this book uses actual case studies to illustrate the fact that every child and young person is an individual who deserves a holistic view of their educational provision."

Dr Sue Soan, Senior Lecturer, Canterbury Christ Church University

"An accessible and informative read about an often overlooked group of learners. Presented in an engaging format through the use of real children's experiences, this book provides an excellent guidance and reference point for helping to identify and better understand learners with complex needs and how to maximise their considerable potential in the classroom."

Ellen Sargeant, Primary School Teacher

"This is a most authoritative and timely book and I liked the format. A book written by experts in an easy to absorb language. Essential reading for school leaders, Heads of Inclusion, SENCOs and GATCOs. Follow this 'yellow brick road' and it really will raise the school's standards of achievement. Inclusion, coproduction and an emphasis on strengths – a recipe for society as a whole."

Professor Diane Montgomery, Professor Emerita at Middlesex University

The School Handbook for Dual and Multiple Exceptionality

The School Handbook for Dual and Multiple Exceptionality (DME) offers a range of practical strategies to support SENCOs, GATCOs, school leaders and governors in developing effective provision for children that have both High Learning Potential and Special Educational Needs or Disabilities. Building on the principles of child-centred provision and coproduction, it provides useful tips on developing the school workforce to better identify and meet the needs of learners with DME.

Relevant for learners in primary, secondary or specialist settings, the book focuses on ways of meeting individual needs and maximising personal and academic outcomes. It includes:

- An explanation of what DME is and why we should care about it
- Practical advice and guidance for SENCOs, GATCOs and school leaders on developing the school workforce
- A discussion of the strategic role of governors and trustees in the context of DME
- Suggested approaches to ensure effective coproduction between families and professionals
- Case studies exploring the experiences of learners with DME
- Sources of ongoing support and resources from professional organisations and key influencers

This book will be beneficial to all those teachers, school leaders, SENCOs, GATCOs, governors and trustees looking to support learners by identifying and understanding DME. It recognises the central role that leaders and governors play in setting the inclusive ethos of a school and suggests ways for schools to ensure that all learners have the opportunity to meet their full potential.

Denise Yates has worked in education and training for more than 35 years with a range of vulnerable groups, including ex-offenders, children with Special Educational Needs and young people at risk of offending. For ten years, Denise was Chief Executive of the national charity Potential Plus UK (formerly The National Association for Gifted Children). In 2017, Denise left Potential Plus UK to follow her twin passions of raising awareness of mental health issues and of children with Dual and Multiple Exceptionality. Denise is currently Chair of Miricyl, a new charity which focuses on the prevention of mental illness amongst children and young people, a Trustee of The Potential Trust, a charitable trust which supports more able children from low income backgrounds and Chair of GT Voice, the UK network for organisations and individuals interested in supporting children and young people with High Learning Potential. Denise is also Non-Executive Director of the Nisai Education Trust and a Fellow of the RSA.
@DeniseYates_

Adam Boddison is Chief Executive of nasen, the National Association for Special Educational Needs. Adam is Chair of the Whole School SEND Consortium, a Trustee of The Potential Trust, a National Leader of Governance and a Director of The Active Learning Trust, which includes primary, secondary and special schools. Adam was formerly Director of the Centre for Professional Education at the University of Warwick and Academic Principal for IGGY (a global educational social network for gifted teenagers). Adam is a Visiting Professor at the University of Wolverhampton and is a qualified clinical hypnotherapist.
@adamboddison

Helping Everyone Achieve ■■■

nasen is a professional membership association that supports all those who work with or care for children and young people with special and additional educational needs. Members include SENCOs, school leaders, governors/trustees, teachers, teaching assistants, support workers, other educationalists, students and families.

nasen supports its members through policy documents, peer-reviewed academic journals, its membership magazine *nasen Connect*, publications, professional development courses, regional networks and newsletters. Its website contains more current information such as responses to government consultations.

nasen's published documents are held in very high regard both in the UK and internationally.

For a full list of titles see: www.routledge.com/nasen-spotlight/book-series/FULNASEN

Other titles published in association with the National Association for Special Educational Needs (nasen):

The School Handbook for Dual and Multiple Exceptionality
Denise Yates and Adam Boddison
2020/pb: 978-0-367-36958-3

Creating Multi-sensory Environments: Practical Ideas for Teaching and Learning, Revised Edition
Christopher Davies
2020/pb: 978-0-415-57330-6

Dyslexia and Inclusion: Classroom Approaches for Assessment, Teaching and Learning
Gavin Reid
2019/pb: 978-1-138-48749-9

Using an Inclusive Approach to Reduce School Exclusion: A Practitioner's Handbook
Tristan Middleton and Lynda Kay
2019/pb: 978-1-138-31691-1

Supporting SLCN in children with ASD in the Early Years: A Practical Resource for Professionals
Jennifer Warwick
2019/pb: 978-1-138-36950-4

How to be a Brilliant SENCO: Practical Strategies for Developing and Leading Inclusive Provision
Helen Curran
2019/pb: 978-1-138-48966-0

Successfully Teaching and Managing Children with ADHD: A resource for SENCOs and teachers, 2ed
Fintan O'Regan
2018/pb: 978-0-367-11010-9

Brain Development and School: Practical Classroom Strategies to Help Pupils Develop Executive Function
Pat Guy
2019/pb: 978-1-138-49491-6

The School Handbook for Dual and Multiple Exceptionality

High Learning Potential with Special Educational Needs or Disabilities

Denise Yates and Adam Boddison

Routledge
Taylor & Francis Group

LONDON AND NEW YORK

First published 2020
by Routledge
2 Park Square, Milton Park, Abingdon, Oxon OX14 4RN

and by Routledge
52 Vanderbilt Avenue, New York, NY 10017

Routledge is an imprint of the Taylor & Francis Group, an informa business

British Library Cataloguing-in-Publication Data
A catalogue record for this book is available from the British Library

Library of Congress Cataloging-in-Publication Data
Names: Yates, Denise, author. | Boddison, Adam, 1981- author.
Title: The school handbook for dual and multiple exceptionality: high
    learning potential with special educational needs or disabilities /
    Denise Yates and Adam Boddison.
Description: Abingdon, Oxon ; New York, NY : Routledge, 2020. | Series:
    NASEN spotlight | Includes bibliographical references and index.
Identifiers: LCCN 2019056544 (print) | LCCN 2019056545 (ebook) |
    ISBN 9780367369576 (hardback) | ISBN 9780367369583 (paperback) |
    ISBN 9780429352041 (ebook)
Subjects: LCSH: Gifted children—Education—Great Britain. | Children with
    disabilities—Education—Great Britain. | Special education—Great
    Britain—Administration.
Classification: LCC LC3997.G7 Y37 2020 (print) | LCC LC3997.G7 (ebook) |
    DDC 371.95—dc23
LC record available at https://lccn.loc.gov/2019056544
LC ebook record available at https://lccn.loc.gov/2019056545

ISBN: 978-0-367-36957-6 (hbk)
ISBN: 978-0-367-36958-3 (pbk)
ISBN: 978-0-429-35204-1 (ebk)

Typeset in Helvetica
by Swales & Willis, Exeter, Devon, UK

Contents

Foreword

Danielle Brown MBE

I am under no illusion how fortunate I am that my early influencers recognised my talents. Their belief in me got me to see what they saw, to understand that my dreams were valid and that I had the ability to achieve them. They supported me through the challenges that living with a disability brings and helped me channel my energy into positive outlets where I could excel.

Strong foundations enable us to succeed and their patience, hard work, unerring positivity and out-of-the box thinking helped facilitate a successful career in sport. I am a two-time Paralympic gold medallist and five-time World Champion in archery. Many of my medals were achieved whilst I was in education, securing the highest GCSE grades in my school and graduating from university with first-class honours in law.

Sport taught me so many incredible lessons – how to take personal responsibility, how to bounce back from failure, and how to turn a crazy goal into a reality. But most of all it taught me to value myself. The low confidence and self-worth I suffered in my teenage years were destructive on another level entirely and, if left unchecked, had the real potential to cost me my ambitions. Being able to work with children and young people, to put something back and offer them the same belief that my team gave to me is a privilege and something I am incredibly passionate about.

I am delighted to be a patron for nasen who make a real difference to children and young people with SEND. Becoming the best versions of ourselves is something that we can all achieve. It's something that we all deserve to achieve, and sometimes we need a little extra support on that journey. Our differences can become our USPs if we are taught in the right way and given opportunities to succeed.

But the reality is that we live in an intersectional world, and understanding Dual and Multiple Exceptionality (DME) in children helps them nurture their talents and work on their challenges in order to reach their full potential. I thoroughly enjoyed reading this book; it's a thought-provoking guide filled with valuable messages and practical strategies. Through case studies and comprehensive analysis you are able to understand the best approach to first recognise DME in pupils and then develop the right strategy to support them.

I particularly resonated with the strengths-based approach adopted by the authors. Success does not come from the absence of weakness, but from making your strengths stronger. Nor is it a one-person mission. We are only as strong as our weakest link and the people around us often determine the extent of our successes – or failures! Focusing on what we can do rather than what we can't and having this recognised by those around us instils confidence and self-worth, both of which are key to growth in many areas.

We can draw many parallels between educators and coaches. The best coaches I had weren't decorated with national qualifications, but were the ones who understood how I operated, my motivators and were able to adapt their approach to meet my needs. This individualised performance plan enabled me to get the most out of myself as both a person and an athlete, promoting better mental health and allowing me to excel in the areas I was good at whilst supporting me in the areas where I needed it.

The concept of coproduction discussed in this book is something that the world of sport has been getting right for years. Seeing all parties as equal stakeholders and creating opportunities for each person to contribute and take ownership allows for more innovative ideas, a better use of resources and bigger buy in. When everybody feels part of the process it prompts action and creates an inclusive culture – and when you get this right we see a much greater impact.

The School Handbook for Dual and Multiple Exceptionality offers a fantastic insight into DME and how to ensure effective provision in schools so that children with both High Learning Potential and Special Educational Needs or Disabilities can flourish.

We all have the power to make a difference and nobody should be left behind.

After all, education drives change.

Danielle

Introduction

This book is designed to be a practical resource that can be used in several ways. It can be read through from beginning to end for those who want to understand more about Dual and Multiple Exceptionality (DME) from a range of perspectives. For those with roles in schools, it may be helpful to use the book as a reference guide, accessing the chapters that are most relevant to your specific area of responsibility.

As is often the case within education, there are many acronyms and there is a breadth of specialist language. To support the reader, we have produced a glossary within the appendices covering the key terminology used in this book, which we hope will make the text accessible to as wide an audience as possible. If you are unfamiliar with educational acronyms and terminology, you may find it useful to look at the glossary before you read the book. In relation to terminology, we are conscious that there are variations and inconsistencies across the education sector and across different countries. In this book, we have used some terms and acronyms interchangeably to reflect this diversity, such as Special Educational Needs and Disabilities/Special Educational Needs (SEN/SEND), Autistic Spectrum Condition/Autistic Spectrum Disorder, learner/pupil/child. In Wales and Scotland, the terms 'additional learning needs' and 'additional support needs' are used, which are much broader than SEN/SEND, but the principles discussed in this book are equally applicable. There are other examples, too, and we hope that the reader will understand our decision to use a broader range of language.

There are some features of the book that it may be useful to know about before you start reading. Each chapter begins with a quote and an outline of the subsections within the chapter. Within the chapters, we have sought to break up the text with lists, diagrams and tables to ensure that information is available in a range of formats for the reader. We offer a note of caution here that such lists should not be used in isolation as check-lists, since every child is individual and not everything in this book will apply to every child. The reader should take some time to understand the nuances and complexities of DME and then think about how their knowledge can be applied in a particular context. At the end of each chapter, two myths about DME are shared and there are ten myths altogether spread across the book. A full list of the myths is included in the appendices for you to use as a wall-poster in the classroom or elsewhere.

Ultimately, this book is about individual children and so within each of Chapters 1 to 4, we introduce you to a number of real children with DME. The intention here is that you develop a concept in your mind about how a learner with DME might appear in practice, so you know what to look for within your own context. Pseudonyms have been used to protect the identities of the children, their families and their schools. In Chapter 5 you can read the full story for each child and find out more about how their schools approached identification and provision.

Last, we would like to clarify that this book is intended to promote inclusion. By inclusion, we are not referring to the place in which children receive their education, but rather the approach that is taken. We believe that inclusion can occur anywhere (mainstream school, special school, alternative provision, home education) or in any setting if the needs of the individual are at the heart of decisions about provision. Learners with DME are not a homogenous group, so what is inclusive for one child may not be inclusive for another.

We hope that this book serves as a useful guide in maximising inclusion in your school.

The underpinning principles in this book

This book is about DME children and young people; who they are, how to support them and why it matters. If implemented in the right way, the underpinning principles in this book can help to better meet the learning differences of a group of children and young people, which are often misidentified or not identified at all. Effective identification and provision have the potential to have a major positive impact on individual achievement levels and school performance. It could lead to a reduction in some of the negative consequences of failure in school and in our society as a whole, with improvements in exclusion rates and the rates of offending and reoffending. Effective identification and provision can also lead to increased motivation, resilience and self-esteem in children and young people.

Five underpinning principles have been identified for teachers, SENCOs, GATCOs, school leaders, governors and trustees:

1. **Coproduction is at the heart of effective DME provision** – it is essential that meaningful child-centred strategies involving parents/carers, teachers and pupils as equal partners are at the heart of implementing DME provision.
2. **SEND and High Learning Potential (HLP) can co-occur** – all school-based professionals must recognise, believe and support through their work the view that SEND and HLP can co-occur and that this is called Dual and Multiple Exceptionality (DME). This includes everyone from the board of governors or trustees in a school to the senior leadership team, SENCOS, GATCOS, teachers and all those professionals working in and for the school.
3. **DME provision is inclusive, not exclusive** – DME should be seen as part of a strategy for inclusivity within the school. The apparent strengths of the child or young person should not be a barrier to having needs met or potential fulfilled. Some schools are already merging SEND and HLP into strategies for inclusion, which are based on promoting the strengths of the child or young person and using these to support their challenges, and this inclusive approach should be considered by all schools in the future.
4. **Getting DME provision right benefits wider society** – if done in the right way, effective DME provision not only benefits one child, one class or one school. It can have a major impact on those issues which impact on our society as a whole. Getting it right for learners with DME would raise educational outcomes within a group that has traditionally underachieved. Rather than being failed by the education system and becoming dependent on society, learners with DME have the potential to be major contributors to society. Getting it right has the potential to improve economic value in our society as these children and young people have a better chance of building on their strengths to get the jobs they want and to contribute to this country's economy positively. It can also have a positive impact on the individual's mental health and well-being, improving their self-esteem and enabling them to form positive relationships with others. All of this would have a beneficial impact on social mobility, ensuring every child has a chance of progressing regardless of their background.

   Conversely, ignoring DME may have an impact on a range of issues from school exclusion and self-exclusion, offending and reoffending behaviour to mental health issues including self-harm and suicide. Addressing DME as part of a wider government strategy is therefore essential.
5. **Effective DME provision is replicable, scalable and sustainable** – some schools in the UK are already addressing the issue of DME as part of their inclusion strategy but we are a long way behind other countries, such as the USA, Australia and New Zealand. DME provision should have the potential to be replicated and scaled-up to meet the needs of different communities and schools, including special schools, free schools and multi-academy trusts. Models of good practice need to be developed to show what is possible and how including DME as part of an inclusion strategy can be sustainable given existing structures and resource levels.

1 What is DME and why should we care?

She is refusing to go to school, and we think it is a behavioural issue, but the parents say that she is afraid of failure and highly anxious. We put her in the bottom set to support her.

(Teacher, prior to knowing about DME)

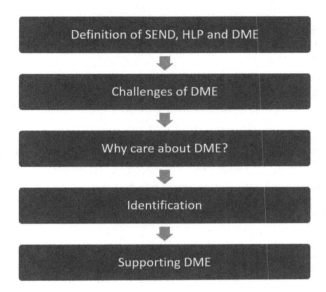

Figure 1.1

This book is about potential; more specifically, how to identify, support and nurture High Learning Potential (HLP) in a child or young person with one or more Special Educational Needs or Disabilities. A child or young person who has a gift or talent in one or more areas as well as a special need or disability is called Dual and Multiple Exceptional (or DME for short). In some countries, this individual may be referred to as being Twice Exceptional or 2e or Gifted with Learning Difficulties (GLD).

DME may not be a term many professionals have come across, whether they are a SEND Co-ordinator or a Gifted and Talented Co-ordinator (GATCO), and yet it is a term which is important to both disciplines as well as class teachers and other professionals in school including the senior leadership team and the board of governors or trustees who lead the school.

Definition of SEND

Those professionals who work in the area of SEND or who have some experience of these issues in the classroom or beyond should be familiar with the definition of SEND.

According to the Department for Education and the Department of Health SEND Code of Practice (DfE and DoH, 2015), a child or young person has Special Educational Needs if they have a learning difficulty or disability which calls for special educational provision to be made for him or her. A child of compulsory school age or a young person has a learning difficulty or disability if he or she has:

(a) significantly greater difficulty in learning than the majority of others of the same age; or
(b) a disability which prevents or hinders them from making use of educational facilities of a kind generally provided for others of the same age in mainstream schools or mainstream post-16 institutions.

Special Educational Needs and Disabilities are grouped under four broad areas:

1. **Communication and interaction** – children and young people with speech, language or communication issues. Specific learning difficulties such as dyslexia or a physical or sensory impairment such as hearing loss may also lead to communication difficulties. Children and young people with an Autism Spectrum Condition may have difficulties with communication, social interaction and imagination. In addition, they may be easily distracted or upset by certain stimuli, have problems with change to familiar routines or have difficulties with their co-ordination and fine-motor functions.

2. **Cognition and learning** – children and young people with learning difficulties may learn at a slower pace than other children and may have greater difficulty than their peers in acquiring basic literacy or numeracy skills or in understanding concepts, even with appropriate differentiation, including dyslexia, dyscalculia and dyspraxia. However, those with cognition and learning issues may also have other difficulties such as speech and language delay, low self-esteem, low levels of concentration and under-developed social skills.

   This definition of cognition and learning issues can be difficult to demonstrate for children and young people with DME, many of whom are learning at age-appropriate levels and pace. The key is not to evaluate their learning difficulty in relation to that of their class peers but in relation to what and how they are capable of otherwise learning with the right support. The risk is that children and young people with DME can appear to be operating at or above average within their peer group. As shall be seen later, particularly in some of the case studies, whilst this can be difficult to measure, it is not impossible to identify and provide for.

   In circumstances where DME is unidentified, children are at risk of developing additional Special Educational Needs, particularly social, emotional and mental health issues. They may then need additional support in these areas, even where it did not present as a Special Educational Need in the first instance but arose from inaccurate identification within the broad area of cognition and learning.

3. **Social, emotional and mental health** – children and young people who have difficulties with their social and emotional development may have immature social skills and find it difficult to make and keep healthy relationships. Resulting issues can range from being withdrawn or socially isolated to having disruptive or challenging behaviour. This can lead to emotional health issues such as self-harm, eating disorders, trichotillomania, anxiety or depression. Some children and young people may also have other recognised disorders such as attention deficit hyperactivity disorder (ADHD), attachment disorder, anxiety disorder or, more rarely, conditions such as schizophrenia or bipolar disorder.

4. **Sensory and/or physical** – children or young people with vision impairment (VI), hearing impairment (HI) or multisensory impairment (MSI) or other physical difficulties would fall into this broad area.

Many children and young people have difficulties that fit clearly into one of these areas. Increasingly, learners have needs that span two or more areas, which is known as comorbidity or co-occurring needs, but for others the precise nature of their need may not be clear at the outset. This can often be the case with a child or young person who has DME.

Box 1.1 An introduction to Alex

Alex was a highly verbal child; speaking in whole sentences by the age of 2. By 3 he could tell his family members stories which tapped into his vivid imagination and which left them in no doubt what a bright boy they had. He went to a local private nursery setting on a part-time basis and they confirmed what his parents had thought when his key worker talked to them about his intellectual boredom being a possible reason for the sudden onset of his misbehaviour. His key worker recommended that he should be moved to primary school as soon as possible to get greater intellectual stimulation, which his parents did.

At school, he enjoyed anything which enabled him to talk and use his imagination. However, he struggled at the outset with his handwriting and organisational skills and avoided reading wherever possible. His maths ability was also extremely variable. For example, he struggled with mental maths, but he was extremely good at anything which involved visual or spatial maths.

His teachers could not understand how, when he was asked a question, he usually knew the answer but when he had to write anything down or concentrate on something in which he wasn't interested, he did not engage. Various teachers put it down to everything from laziness to poor behaviour to lack of ability.

As he grew older, Alex became the class clown and was good at playing his teachers and parents off against each other to get out of homework which, when he had to do it, was a nightmare at home and could take the better part of a day to complete. His parents found that if he dictated it to them it was fine and then they dictated it back to him in 'chunks' over the course of the day. Sometimes this lasted into the evening as he grew tired quickly and found it difficult to write for long periods.

By the time he was 8, his parents were extremely worried about Alex. They began to research everything about various Special Educational Needs, looking for answers about what was going on in school. He could read when he set his mind to it, although he wasn't a natural reader. In addition, providing maths was explained visually or spatially, his only issues seemed to be with lack of interest and ability to process information. Lack of organisational skills was still a problem but that was put down to it 'just being Alex'.

In secondary school, Alex remained the class clown and his parents were regularly contacted by his teachers 'because of his sense of humour' and imaginative antics. However, what they didn't realise until many years later was that he was also bullied by the other boys because he did not like things like football, preferring music and drama.

To build on his strengths and his interests, his parents paid for music lessons and a drama club in the local community and these were recognised when he was placed on the 'Gifted and Talented Register' at school. This amused Alex because, from the age of about 8 or 9, his self-esteem in terms of his schoolwork had been rapidly decreasing, making school in most cases a negative experience for him. For example, when asked who was better than he was at maths he answered, 'an ant'.

Alex's full story can be found in Chapter 5.

Definition of HLP

Those individuals who work with children and young people who are clever or who have one or more gifts or talents will know that there are many terms and definitions in use currently, or which have been used in the past, to define these children.

The variety of terms for these individuals is recognised by Freeman in the seminal work 'Educating the Very Able' (Freeman, 1998), a government-commissioned report published just before the launch of the government's gifted and talented programme. Here she refers to 'the troublesome word "gifted", with its implications of gifts bestowed intact from on high'. However, 'gifted and talented' was the term chosen by the government for its national programme and this continued to be used for many years after the programme ended and is still in use in many schools across the country.

This repeated failure to agree to standard terminology and definitions which everyone could use, and which were not seen as elitist, contributed to the closure of the only national government programme in England to support these children. Following this closure of the government's gifted and talented programme in the mid-2000s (and after a number of years without a co-ordinated government policy) the most popular of these terms are or have been:

More able, Most Able or High Attainers – these are the current terms used by Ofsted and the Department of Education and focus on 'those who have abilities in one or more academic subjects such as mathematics or English'.

More/Most Able – this term either on its own or with gifted and talented was inserted by schools and government and reflects the unease which many people felt at the term 'gifted and talented' which was seen as 'elitist' and 'not reflecting the education situation in many schools'. More/most able (which are often used interchangeably) was defined as those who have abilities in one or more subject areas and the capacity for or ability to demonstrate high levels of performance. Thus, someone could be academic because they worked hard and applied themselves rather than because they had an innate ability in one or more subjects.

More Able and Talented – this was used by the Welsh Government to show pupils who are more able across the curriculum as well as those who show aptitudes in one or more specific areas such as art, sport, music or drama. It also includes pupils who may additionally show exceptional teamworking, leadership or entrepreneurial skills.

Gifted and Talented – this is the term still in use in many schools in England, often with gifted taken to mean academic ability and talented those other practical subjects such as sport and artistic performance. As part of its gifted and talented programme, the Department for Children, Schools and Families (as the Department for Education was then called) defined gifted and talented as 'Children with one or more abilities developed to a level significantly ahead of their peers (or with the potential to develop those abilities)' (DCSF, 2008).

This picks up the fact that the government at the time recognised that many gifted and talented children were, in fact, underachieving, despite having the ability to achieve high results in school.

There are countless other terms and definitions in schools across the country reflecting, perhaps, the unease amongst professionals and sometimes parents, carers, children and young people in using the term 'gifted and talented'.

One term which appears to be gaining traction in schools and which is adopted in this book is High Learning Potential (sometimes shortened to HLP). This term was first adopted in 2009 by the national charity Potential Plus UK to address these and other concerns with the terminology in current use (Potential Plus UK, 2018).

Whilst as professionals, the attainment of every child or young person is important, the term 'High Learning Potential' is also about the ability of these individuals to achieve. Many of these children, particularly when their DME is not recognised or supported, fail to achieve what they are capable of and can often become frustrated and lack self-confidence in their abilities.

Potential Plus UK defines High Learning Potential as those children and young people who have one or more of the following attributes:

- exceptional abilities;
- the ability to attain highly, but who, for whatever reason, are not attaining at that level;
- who are dual or multiple exceptional (high ability with a special educational need or disability);
- who are profoundly gifted (approximately 0.01% of learners)

This appears to cover both ability and attainment, whilst recognising that many of these children and young people are not attaining the levels expected, including for reasons of DME.

What is DME?

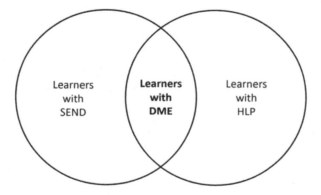

Figure 1.2 Diagrammatical representation of DME, SEND and HLP.

In the recent nasen-commissioned publication, *Dual and Multiple Exceptionality: The Current State of Play*, the definition of DME is taken from one of the UK's leading academic researchers in this area, Professor Diane Montgomery (Ryan and Waterman, 2018, p. 2). She gives the following definition:

In the gifted education field, double or dual and multiple exceptionality (2E and DME) are terms used to describe those who are intellectually very able (gifted) or who have a talent (a special gift in a performance or skill area) and in addition to this, have a special educational need (SEN) such as dyslexia, or Asperger's syndrome.

(Montgomery, 2015, p. ix)

The national approach to SEN policy in England has now broadened to include disabilities and this is known as SEND (Special Educational Needs or Disabilities). It is therefore appropriate to ensure the definition of DME includes not just those with SEN, but also those individuals with a recognised disability, where that disability impacts on their learning.

SENCOs will no doubt be familiar with the term 'dual exceptionality' or comorbidity where two Special Educational Needs or Disabilities interact with each other but are separate. Multiple exceptionality is where more than two Special Educational Needs or Disabilities interact. DME occurs where one of those Special Educational Needs is HLP.

Box 1.2 An introduction to Thea

As soon as Thea went into reception class, she said that she felt 'different'. She was extremely perceptive for her age and emotionally mature. However, this feeling of 'difference' was making her miserable. According to her parents, she lay awake for hours at night, feeling anxious and unable to sleep; and repeatedly asked her parents what was wrong with her.

Thea attended reception at the local state primary school, where she was quickly put onto the SEND register. Thea's difficulties were seen as 'deficits' and her social situation was regarded as being due to social and communication difficulties.

However, Thea's parents saw a child who communicated well with older children and adults. She was also a child who thrived with a combination of challenge and careful support. This support enabled her to access more complex problems and then, with the right encouragement, she was even more willing to go out of her 'comfort zone' and attempt things that she found more difficult such as physical activities.

Her parents also recognised that Thea was highly sensitive, not only emotionally but also physically. She was easily overwhelmed, and it was felt by her parents that this was clouding the school's judgement of her actual academic ability.

Thea's full story can be found in Chapter 5.

What challenges do children and young people with DME face?

Many children or young people with SEND are achieving great things in school. Many have also been identified and are receiving the right support to meet their needs. Likewise, it is also recognised that many children with HLP are being supported to achieve the highest grades, whilst recognising that, without appropriate support, they may not work to the level of their capabilities.

Nevertheless, a pupil with DME can face particular challenges with both their Special Educational Needs or Disabilities *and* their HLP which can result in chronic underachievement and low self-esteem. This can lead to a variety of issues including exclusion, self-exclusion, offending behaviour, poor mental health and related factors such as self-harm and suicide.

Common challenges include:

1. Their strengths compensate for or even conceal a SEND, making it extremely difficult to identify correctly both the existence of or the extent of the issues faced by the child or young person. Sometimes these can go unnoticed for years or even for a lifetime.
2. Their needs or abilities can be misidentified or misinterpreted as something else, making it extremely difficult for professionals to provide the right support.
3. Where a need is identified, emphasis can be placed on supporting this to the exclusion of the child or young person's HLP, which also needs to be recognised and supported.
4. Typical measures to support a learning difficulty or disability may not be successful for a child who also has HLP.
5. Where the child or young person's strengths are identified, traditional gifted and talented or SEND programmes may not be suitable without appropriate adaptation as they are reliant upon basic or advanced skills being in place.
6. The current emphasis in education is often on children and young people achieving the national expectations for their year. However, assessment may show that the child or young person is achieving these expectations or is even slightly above average, even when they have a recognised SEND. If the level at which they *could* be working is not identified and the difference

between the two is not seen as a Special Education Need to be supported, the impact on their self-confidence and emotional health can be significant, leading to problems such as self-harm, eating disorders, offending behaviour, exclusion or self-exclusion from school.

Arguably, the biggest challenges facing children and young people with DME are poor self-esteem or lack of confidence about what they can do. Their own questioning about whether they have any abilities at all can be exacerbated by both parents and professionals who may not see or understand the effort that these children put in to appearing 'average'. This can cause tension both at home and at school, with these children often labelled 'lazy' for failing to meet the standards expected or for seeking to avoid challenge at school with homework or even in exams.

A clearer way of representing the different types of situation when supporting and challenging children and young people with DME can be seen in Figure 1.3. The identification of the following four DME pupil profiles provides a useful outline to support understanding of the issue:

- **Type 1** – HLP recognised, SEND unrecognised: their ability enables them to 'get by', compensating for their Special Educational Needs through use of their advanced abilities.
- **Type 2** – HLP unrecognised, SEND recognised: often labelled for what they cannot do, rather than what they can, often failing to achieve in school where they can display negative or disruptive behaviours.
- **Type 3** – HLP unrecognised, SEND unrecognised: each aspect masks the other. This is the group most at risk of underachievement, since the needs are never addressed and the potential is never realised.
- **Type 4** – HLP recognised, SEND recognised; these children/young people receive both the support and challenge they need.

The aim of teaching children and young people with DME should be to move every pupil to Type 4 of the matrix in Figure 1.3 so that both their SEND and their HLP are recognised and supported and they can receive the challenge they need.

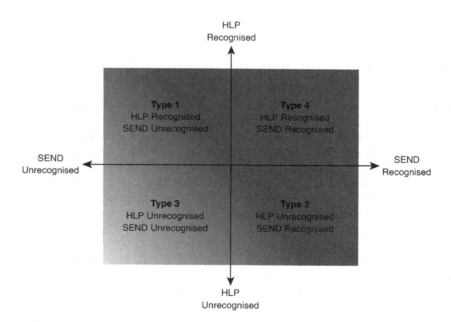

Figure 1.3 DME matrix.

All of this means that there is a high likelihood that many children and young people with DME will be underachieving with a potential impact in other areas such as mental health needs, truancy, behavioural issues and lifelong low self-esteem. This broader set of consequences is likely to put additional financial and time pressures on the wider support systems. In *Raising the Achievement of All Pupils within an Inclusive Setting*, Montgomery stresses the interaction between three factors in determining different patterns of underachievement and exceptionality (Wallace et al., 2010):

Culture – e.g. the individual's background, their socio-economic status and how this supports or fails to support the child or young person with DME.

Personal issues – the abilities, Special Educational Needs or Disabilities of the individual and how they themselves cope with them and their personal qualities. Motivation, personality and resilience can have a major impact on how a child or young person with DME copes. These are all significant contributors to how learners respond to everything from failure and set-back to being put in care, being ostracised in the classroom or being excluded from school.

Pedagogy – the teaching methods, behaviour management and way the teacher responds to the child with DME and their circumstances. This is critical if the child or young person is to achieve their best. Inappropriate teaching, such as being placed in the lowest set to do remedial work, can create significant impediments to the learning and progress of the child with DME and should be avoided.

Getting it wrong can lead to a significant drain on financial and other resources, such as time, on the part of teaching staff and others involved in the process, for example mental health professionals, as well as personal impact on the individual in terms of lifelong low self-esteem, aspirations and mental health issues.

Conversely, the teacher who just 'gets it' and responds to the learner's sense of humour and often sophisticated insights on the world, can reap rewards in their learning and behaviour, increased resilience and positive attitude.

Teachers and other professionals who enjoy working with DME pupils will often recognise and respond to their quirky senses of humour, creativity and divergent ways of thinking. Approaching DME provision in this way can be beneficial for the pupil, the teacher and the class. However, different teaching staff may elicit different responses from the individual pupil and this, coupled with the increased difficulty of the work as the child or young person progresses through the school, can have a detrimental impact upon them and their achievement levels.

According to Linda Silverman of the Gifted Development Center in the USA, in her book *Giftedness 101*:

> In most cases, their highly abstract reasoning enables 2e [DME] children to compensate sufficiently to get by with at least low average grades during their first years of school; but with each year level, their struggle intensifies. They must work harder to maintain passing grades … Their gargantuan efforts are often rewarded by their being considered not good enough for gifted programmes and too good to qualify for accommodations. Catch 22!
>
> (Silverman, 2013)

How many children with DME are there in the UK?

It is difficult to give an accurate calculation of the number of children with DME in the UK as these figures are not consistently held by schools or local or central government. Nonetheless, in the 2018 report on DME commissioned by nasen, its authors suggested that between 40,000 and 80,000 children and young people in the education system in England are Dual or Multiple Exceptional. Using figures on Special Educational Needs drawn by the government from the January 2019 school census, this represents between one in 16 and one in 33 respectively of all SEND pupils aged 5–18 in the school population (DfE, 2019a).

However, even these approximations may underestimate the scale of the issue, not only because they do not include comparative figures for the other nations in the UK, but they are also likely to underestimate the scale of the issue itself. For example, not all DME pupils are likely to have been identified as SEND. Many of them have 'disappeared in the system' and are seen neither as pupils with SEND nor as pupils with HLP (Type 3 from the DME matrix).

According to 'The Timpson Review of School Exclusion', 46.7% of those pupils receiving permanent exclusions (3,362) and 44.9% of all fixed term exclusions had Special Educational Needs (Timpson, 2019). A significant proportion of these may be unidentified pupils with DME. Another group of learners not being educated in schools are those in home education.

A briefing paper on home education in England estimated that the number of home-educated children and young people in 2018 was between 53,000 and 58,000 but that this was rising (Foster and Danechi, 2019). This is only an estimate as data on the number of home-educated children and young people is not collected centrally. Whilst some of these may have been excluded from school or 'off-rolled' so that they can be educated at home, even this may underestimate the scale of the issues both in terms of its focus on England and because some parents and carers choose home education 'under the radar' rather than sending their child to school at all. Some of these children and young people are likely to be DME pupils who do not 'fit' the classic school model.

Finally, some pupils with DME may find themselves outside the traditional education system, either within the community or elsewhere. For example, the Youth Justice Statistics for England and Wales, report that for 2017/18, 22,996 sentences were given in court to children and young people aged 10–17 years old (MoJ, 2019). This resulted in 1,585 custodial sentences and an average population in youth custody of 894 (June 2019). It is recommended that further research work is done in this area, however it is believed that a significant proportion of the children and young people involved in the youth custody system will have DME.

This view is corroborated, if only on a small scale, by the report, 'Releasing Potential' (NAGC, 2012), which was based on research carried out in one young offender institute in 2011.

This report suggested that many of these children or young people had SEND, HLP or DME which had gone unidentified either at school or within the Youth Justice System and that addressing these issues could help to divert them away from crime. According to the research:

> **Boredom** was described as the most common circumstance surrounding recent offences. 78% of young people truanted from a pupil referral unit due to boredom.

> **Underachievement** had led learners to avoid school, especially when coupled with a learning difficulty. 46% of offending children were underachievers in education.

> **Truanting**: on any given day 70,000 children are truanting. 81% of the children who had truanted more than ten times from a pupil referral unit will offend.

> **School Exclusion**: 77% of the children or young people had been excluded from school when entering custody. 60% of excluded children reported committing an offence in the past 12 months.

> **Peer pressure**: Many children or young people were reluctant to put in effort and achieve at school as this would isolate them from their friends. Alarmingly, 58% of students in pupil referral units reported that their peer group viewed crime as acceptable.

It would be interesting to carry out further work on the journey of a young person with DME from school to alternative provision to the criminal justice system. It would be particularly useful to evaluate the impact that attributes such as motivation, resilience and personality have on the barriers to achievement of this group.

In his foreword to the report, Lord Ramsbotham, Her Majesty's Chief Inspector of Prisons between 1995 and 2001, stated:

> What is particularly valuable about this report is that, in addition to being a wake-up call to all those involved with offender learning, it is also a wake-up call to government in general. How much better if the talents that currently go unrecognised amongst those in custody, were recognised early enough for their development to prevent offending? If all educational authorities were required to monitor the progress of those with High Learning Potential and make suitable arrangements for that potential to be harnessed, how much senseless waste of talent could be avoided.

Whilst the situation may have changed fundamentally since 2011, many of the concerns raised in the report remain unresolved.

Taking all these figures into account, the number of children with DME in England could be closer to the upper end of 80,000 and even beyond.

Why should professionals care about children with DME?

There are many reasons why all professionals should care about meeting the needs of children with DME, not least to avoid a negative impact on the individual, the school and, ultimately, on society because of the economic and social waste of potential.

As a teacher or other professional, having an unidentified or misidentified child with DME in the classroom can be a frustrating experience. They can disrupt teaching and class cohesion and they can make the professional question their methods and why they are having difficulty getting through to this particular pupil, with a resulting impact on the professional's own self-confidence and self-esteem.

Most professionals care about every pupil and want to see them achieve their best, even when they are frustrated by them. Children with DME can show 'flashes of brilliance' but this may not be backed up with their written work. Alternatively, they might be the first to put up their hand when the teacher asks a question but stop working when they are asked to get involved in teamwork. They may be the class clown with a quirky sense of humour, but they never seem to deliver the goods in terms of their homework, and it is tempting to think that they are lazy. But every good teacher knows that there is something that they are missing. It could be that they have DME.

This argument holds true even for those pupils who seem 'pretty average' and who just get on with their work. Many teachers (and parents or carers) are surprised when they see the results of a child's formal assessment and realise that they have missed their HLP or SEND (or both).

Girls may be particularly at risk of underidentification or misidentification. An analysis of the results of more than 5,500 children and young people who had been assessed at the Gifted Development Center from 1979 to 2007 was undertaken. The key findings were summarised in the article 'What We Have Learned about Gifted Children 1979–2007' (Silverman, 2007). One of the findings was that gifted (and DME) girls and boys have very different coping mechanisms and are likely to face different problems with HLP or DME. As Silverman said in her article:

> gifted girls and gifted boys have different coping mechanisms and are likely to face different problems. Gifted girls hide their abilities and learn to blend in with other children. In elementary school they direct their mental energies into developing social relationships; in junior high school they are valued for their appearance and sociability rather than for their intelligence. Gifted boys are easier to spot, but they are often considered 'immature' and may be held back in school if they cannot socialize with children their own age with whom they have no common interests.
>
> (Silverman, 2007)

This corresponds with what Montgomery in the UK has called 'acting out' and 'acting in'. In responding to frustration that their learning needs are not being met, children and young people with DME can develop social, emotional and mental health difficulties. Some, often (but not exclusively) boys, are more likely to 'act out' their frustration that their needs are not being met. This makes them easier to spot in the classroom, leading to more immediate intervention.

Others in the classroom are more likely to 'act in', internalising their frustration and 'blending in' with other pupils or making efforts to please the teacher through good behaviour. This is supported by more recent findings in the field of autism, which suggests significant underidentification of autism in girls for similar reasons (nasen, 2016).

On the one hand, this can lead to the overidentification of boys in comparison to girls, some researchers estimate by a factor of 4:1. It can also mean that teachers step in with some pupils sooner than with others in terms of behaviour management and direct interventions. On the other hand, the learner's frustration turned inwards can lead to depression and other emotional or health problems where the root cause of the issue (DME) is missed. Neither of these responses is ideal and should be a source of concern and a reason why we should care or bother to get the DME framework right.

Misidentifying, or failing to identify, DME in a child or young person can sometimes cause that pupil to act out their frustration inside or outside the classroom. In certain circumstances, this can lead to permanent exclusion from school, alternative provision or time in young offender institutions. This chain of events can have a significant impact on the future of the individual and on society.

As the child progresses through the school, teachers may be under increasing pressure to put their DME pupils into the right group, set or even in for certain GCSEs or A levels and they may not know what to do for the best. Often, children with DME will respond to higher-level work, particularly if it plays to their strengths and will reject lower-level work which they find too easy. The key is how to enable them to do the higher-level work whilst supporting any relevant Special Educational Need (e.g. speech and language needs). Doing this will have a positive impact on results for both the child and the school. Making them do 'more of the same' will not have a positive effect on their learning, achievement or their self-esteem.

The subject of maths can illustrate this point well. A child with DME who is able in one or more aspects of maths may just 'know the answer' but be unable to show their working out before they progress onto higher-level work. Alternatively, they may be particularly able in one area of maths (e.g. calculation) and yet, because of difficulties in other areas of the subject (e.g. geometry), they may never be allowed to progress further than the basic level and so may never be able to show what they could achieve at higher levels with the right support. This might be particularly problematic for a learner with dyscalculia.

According to the manifesto 'Raise the Bar and Mind the Gap' (Potential Plus UK, 2015), there are several additional reasons why we should care about supporting learners with DME. These include, the need to contribute towards human capital, economic growth and increased social mobility and to ensure that more children and young people are allowed to progress regardless of background or income levels.

Supporting DME pupils is critically important for the UK in terms of its 'brain power' through the utilisation of its natural resources (people) which creates a thriving, innovative and profitable economy, which it would be irresponsible to ignore. Supporting all pupils and enabling them, in every way possible, to 'be the best they can be' gives them more choices in life and the chance, if they want it, to be considered for the best jobs on offer. More importantly, it will help to lay the foundations for their positive mental health and high self-esteem, and make them more able to form positive relationships as they go through life.

How can learners with DME be identified?

DME is probably one of the most difficult areas of Special Educational Needs to identify. To do so, it is important to have evidence of both the learning difficulty or disability and the potential for HLP in order to assess any discrepancies between intellectual ability and actual performance.

The following characteristics are helpful guidance for teaching staff to support the identification of children and young people with DME in the classroom. Remember that every child or young person with DME is an individual and will not exhibit every indicator. This set of indicators is not a check-list, but it is a starting point to help teachers recognise DME where it occurs. Notwithstanding, obtaining information in a variety of different ways from a variety of different sources will enable a more accurate picture of the child or young person to be constructed. Common identifiers include:

Intellectual strengths

- Ability/expertise in at least one specific area;
- flashes of brilliance about a subject or issue;
- an active imagination (verbal or written);
- an extensive vocabulary (verbal or written);
- exceptional comprehension;
- vast knowledge about a subject or an area of interest outside school where there is no pressure to perform;
- good problem-solving skills;
- conceptual thinking;
- high performance in tasks requiring abstract thinking and problem-solving;
- excellent visual or auditory memory;
- creativity outside school;
- ability to take part in broad-ranging discussions.

Academic difficulties

- Test results may be at odds with the knowledge of a subject;
- poor basic skills e.g. handwriting, spelling, writing;

- difficulty with phonics;
- inability to do seemingly simple tasks, but finding more complex tasks easier to do;
- success in either mathematics or language subjects, but challenges in the other;
- poor performance under pressure;
- difficulties in completing tasks with a sequence of steps;
- inattentive at times; often seen as a 'daydreamer'.

Emotional indicators

- Minor failures, which create feelings of major inadequacy or meltdowns;
- unrealistically high or low self-expectations of themselves and what they can do;
- feelings of academic ineptitude;
- confusion about their own abilities in comparison to others;
- strong fear of failure;
- sensitivity to criticism;
- experiences of intense frustration;
- low self-esteem;
- feelings of being different from others;
- poor social skills.

Behaviour

General behaviour issues

- Disorganised;
- poor self-control, particularly when they find something difficult;
- often off-task.

Signs of 'acting out'

- Disruptive in class;
- impulsive;
- can be intensely frustrated at times – sometimes this can spill over into anger or aggression on themselves or others;
- poor self-control spills into anger and frustration;
- creative when making excuses to avoid tasks they find difficult;
- joker in the class; using wits or have a quirky sense of humour to deflect any difficulties they may have;
- parents/carers say child is different at home.

Signs of 'acting in'

- 'Teacher-pleaser';
- unmotivated;
- withdrawn at times;
- poor self-control spills into highly charged emotional outbursts (e.g. crying, running out of class);
- any abilities unrecognised at school;
- parents/carers say their child is different at home.

Not every learner with DME will exhibit all of these traits all of the time. However, for DME to exist, there will likely be the presence of 'flashes of brilliance' or high ability either generally or in one or more specific areas, whilst at the same time something preventing that high ability from being realised – the Special Educational Need or Disability.

Common Special Educational Needs and Disabilities associated with DME include:

- Autistic Spectrum Disorder (or conditions);
- ADHD;
- dyslexia, dysgraphia, dyscalculia;
- VI and HI;
- Sensory Processing Disorder including dyspraxia;
- speech and language delays or impairments;
- social, emotional and mental health issues.

Due to difficulties in identification, a multidimensional approach to identifying DME should be taken. Depending on the age of the child or young person, this involves consulting across the curriculum and looking at discrepancies between subject areas and what is required for different skills. An example of this would be a child who might produce one or two lines for a written essay but who flies in terms of both content and creativity when they type or dictate a piece of homework or produce a presentation on a subject about which they are passionate.

A person outside the school system, such as an educational psychologist, may also be involved to observe the child and carry out an assessment. The results of a standardised reading test and a listening test might show a huge variation in ability – a score on the 90th percentile for listening and the 60th percentile for reading would suggest difficulties in interpreting written things. Summative assessments in art, music, drama and physical education might rate considerably higher in some cases than reading, writing and spelling ages or vice versa.

It is this difference between what the child or young person could achieve and what they are currently achieving, which is the key to identifying DME, regardless of year group or age-related expectations. For example, imagine the situation in which a 10-year-old child is assessed as having the ability to achieve levels of work of a 16-year-old, but they are achieving levels of an 11-year-old. They should not be seen as someone achieving one year above their year group. Rather, they should be viewed as someone who is underachieving by five years and who, with the right support, could finally begin to have the difficulties hindering them reduced so that they achieve their best. Without this support, they are likely to develop social, emotional or mental health difficulties which will need to be additionally supported.

Potential Plus UK has developed an assessment service which specifically looks at issues such as HLP and DME. More than identification, its purpose is to provide a practical action plan for teachers and other professionals as well as parents and carers in how to support a child or young person with DME or HLP at school or at home.

When assessing a child informally, the school would look at a range of different evidence (and certainly more than one or two sources and the more the better), including:

- schoolwork;
- work done at home;
- drawings and paintings;
- parents' comments and assessments;
- classroom observations;
  - observation of ability in reading and/or number and other skills;
  - observation of verbal ability;
  - observation of advanced use of equipment;
  - observation of talents such as sporting abilities, music or drama;
- use of language and communications skills;
- formal reports from either or both the GATCO and/or the SENCO, or equivalent;
- external reports or membership (e.g. Mensa);
- reports from the class teacher and/or subject teacher or reports from other professionals.

This approach of seeking out indicators of DME from across a range of different areas is known as triangulation and this concept is explored in more detail in Chapter 2.

In addition, the professional would look for a range of characteristics associated with a learning difficulty and those associated with high ability. However, this cannot be done in isolation because of the complex interaction between the two.

The list above is far from exhaustive. It depends, to a large extent, on the characteristics of the individual and how they can best be assessed. One size does not fit all, and it might be necessary to adapt the identification criteria to the particular learner, although some elements might be the same across a whole cohort to ensure some degree of standardisation (e.g. SATs results or CATs scores).

Some examples of how schools are navigating the challenges of identification and provision in practice have been outlined in a range of different individual stories in Chapter 5.

How to support the strengths and challenges of a learner with DME

Children and young people with DME may be sensitive, particularly about their perceived lack of abilities. They can also be intense with a tendency towards high (sometimes impossibly so) levels of perfectionism. These traits can mean they have high standards which they feel that they should be able to meet and so they are very hard on themselves when they fail to meet them.

This can be exacerbated when they see their class peers outperforming them at even the simplest of tasks, tasks which they think they should find easy. From a young age, doubts can creep in about their abilities and this can cause deteriorating confidence and self-esteem and the use of coping mechanisms ranging from humour to poor behaviour to simply giving up. Education professionals and parents/carers who focus on the difficulties in the first instance, to the exclusion of their strengths, can reinforce these negative feelings. The resulting damage to their self-image can impact directly on the learner's academic, social and emotional progress.

Focusing instead on the gifts, talents and interests of children with DME (whilst accommodating their difficulties) is more likely to result in improved resilience and the experience of success. If they are given opportunities to develop their strengths, these children can develop a positive image of who they are and a vision of what they might become. This can motivate them and have a positive impact on all their skills, including their areas of difficulty. It can make them more likely to push themselves through these difficult areas because they are now involved in a project they want to complete.

As Fox says in her book *How to Discover and Develop your Child's Strengths: A Guide for Parents and Teachers*:

> Imagine waking up one day and having everyone you encounter understand the ways in which you are unique and extraordinary. What if everyone viewed the things you did as needed contributions and rather than looking at what is wrong with you, people pointed out what is right with you?
>
> (Fox, 2009)

For those who lack social skills and understanding, working with others in the same interest area greatly expands opportunities for positive and productive interaction. Their weaknesses can and must be addressed, but they need to be addressed creatively and preferably in their interest area, not at the expense of the development of their strengths.

This strengths-based approach can be taken forwards on lots of different levels. For example, where a SEND has been identified, turning its attributes from a weakness to something positive about the child or young person can make a major contribution to their self-esteem. An excellent corporate example of the strengths-based approach comes from Auticon International, an IT and compliance consulting business (www.auticon.co.uk), which has companies in the UK, USA, Germany, France, Switzerland and Canada. This company was established in 2011 and all consultants have Autistic Spectrum Condition.

Auticon believes that the attributes of people on the autism spectrum are actually a strength which can be put to good use in their particular industry and, through this, some of the difficulties they might experience can be supported in a win-win-win situation for the employee, the company and the client.

A strengths-based approach does recognise the difficulties which an individual has but also recognises and emphasises the strengths which they may have and uses these as a way into addressing the challenges faced by the individual. Auticon is an excellent example of this in

Table 1.1

Autistic Spectrum Condition Challenge-Based Approach	Autistic Spectrum Condition Strengths-Based Approach
• Lifelong disability • Spectrum condition – will affect different people in different ways • Different strengths and weaknesses • Difficulties communicating with and reacting to people • Poorer processing speeds • Repetitive behaviour • Inability to understand facial expressions • Anxiety • Dislike of change • Sensory overload • Physical and emotional meltdowns in stressful situations	• Attention to detail • Systematic approach to tasks • Logical analysis • Pattern recognition • Error detection • Sustained concentration • Accuracy • Logic • Intense interests in IT, physics, mathematics and technology • Cognitive diversity • New perspectives • Conscientiousness • Loyalty • Sincerity • Ability to evaluate target versus actual results • A genuine awareness for quality

practice. By creating autism-positive work environments and offering tailored and sustained support mechanisms to its autistic employees, they can provide their clients with a means to tap into the amazing talents of autistic people whilst creating rewarding long-term careers for their team.

How to use the strengths-based model to support a child or young person with DME will then depend upon the child or young person themselves; the characteristics of their HLP and SEND, their individual motivations and difficulties or aims and the support which the school is able to provide through the use of such things as technology, curriculum time, interaction of those with similar hobbies, interests or passions and resources. Discussing this or working with the child or young person, their parents and carers and relevant professionals is the best way to devise and implement a strategy which works. Examples of how this has been done in practice are provided in Chapter 5.

How would this approach work in your classroom?

Although there will be variances between individuals at different ages and with a different balance of strengths and weaknesses, information from Dyslexia Scotland provides an excellent illustration of the likely strengths and weaknesses of someone with dyslexia.

Building on the strengths of the child or young person with dyslexia, exploring how these can be used to address areas of difficulty and then supporting these difficulties through, for example, technology can have a positive effect on their motivation, learning and ultimately achievement in school. Without this support, the child or young person with DME can become increasingly frustrated and stressed. This can lead to behavioural issues, mental health issues, low achievement and ultimately disengagement with either learning or with the school itself.

Table 1.2

Dyslexia Challenge-Based Approach	Dyslexia Strengths-Based Approach
• Problems with reading, taking notes and remembering numbers, names and details • Difficulties with timekeeping, managing time and organising work • Problems with written work e.g. spelling and writing • Short-term memory problems • Problems with sequencing • Difficulties giving and following instructions	• Creative • Enjoys practical tasks • Strong visual thinking e.g. sees/thinks in 3D, can visualise structures from plans • Good spatial skills • Good verbal skills • Good at social interaction • Good at problem-solving, thinking 'out-of-the-box' • Seeing the whole picture of an issue or problem

There is no reason why this approach could not be used for every pupil in the class and in partnership with parents, carers and the child or young person themselves. This can provide a positive way forward for embedding inclusion in the classroom and beyond.

Summary

This chapter has outlined what SEND, HLP and DME are, what DME looks like and the challenges a child with DME can face as well as why we should all care about meeting their needs and supporting them to be the best they can be. It has sought to lay the foundations to help all professionals, from the class teacher to boards of governors and trustees, to identify these children. It has also been suggested that a strengths-based approach which prioritises a DME pupil's abilities and interests to help them with the challenges they face will help to improve their self-esteem and motivate them in their learning.

The next chapter focuses in detail on how we can equip the school workforce to meet the challenges of the DME pupil.

Box 1.3 Ten myths of supporting pupils with DME

Myth No. 1: You cannot have a Special Educational Need or Disability and be highly able at the same time.

This is not true. In all schools and settings, whether they are special schools or mainstream schools, primary or secondary schools, state schools, independent schools or specialist or alternative provision, there will be children and young people who, with varying degrees of success, are coping with either their SEND or HLP or both. The challenge for the professional is to identify and support them in the right way.

Myth No. 2: Having HLP makes up for having a Special Educational Need or Disability.

DME pupils can be confusing to teachers and others. They can be hard to identify and sometimes the gifts or talents may be 'cancelled out' by the difficulties they face. This can make the child seem to be 'average' and no matter how well they use their strengths, the SEND still needs to be identified and supported.

2 Equipping the school workforce

We thought the pupil (aged 6) had dyslexia so we had her tested. This showed her dyslexia but also very high ability. We don't know what to do as we have never had to deal with this kind of situation. She is still massively underachieving and struggles with her reading and writing.

(Teacher)

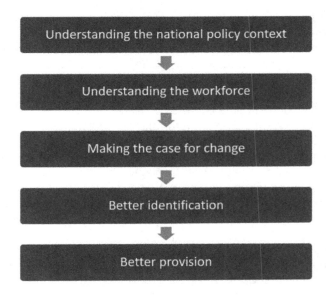

Figure 2.1

This chapter will consider the various elements of a strategic approach to developing the school workforce. An effective approach will ensure that leaders, teachers and support staff are better equipped to understand and meet the needs of learners with DME. There will be an exploration of national policy and suggestions for how professional development can be structured to drive successful workforce development. The principles of effective identification of DME as set out in Chapter 1 will be further built on from the perspective of SENCOs and GATCOs being better positioned to support their colleagues to meet the needs of individual learners.

National policy context

A major challenge in positioning DME within the wider context of national policy is that it is rarely explicitly mentioned and when it is, it is often as a smaller part of a wider initiative. There have been several phases of education policy in England where DME has come briefly to the fore in this way and this has typically been under the banner of gifted and talented provision.

The introduction of grammar schools in 1944 was premised on separating those with academic potential and those without, but even then it was done under the banner of social mobility with a view that talent could be nurtured in those from disadvantaged backgrounds. Over time, gifted and talented initiatives have been repeatedly charged with elitism (Casey and Koshy, 2013) and so DME appears to have suffered a similar fate.

The *Excellence in Cities* initiative that began in 1999 and NAGTY (the National Academy for Gifted and Talented Youth) that ran from 2002 to 2007, both drove school leaders to identify their most able learners, thereby making it easier to recognise those learners with DME. Both initiatives led to and were part of the era of *Every Child Matters* and a sector-wide focus on personalised learning, which was driven by the Labour Party Schools Minister, David Miliband. This was somewhat different to previous initiatives in that it was about every individual child being given the opportunity to reach their full potential.

Gifted and talented education policy was positioned within the principles of 'equality of opportunity' and the 'distribution of rewards according to merit' (Casey and Koshy, 2013). To tackle any accusations of elitism, the government launched a widening participation strategy and the Aimhigher programme, both of which were vehicles for social mobility targeted at bright learners from disadvantaged backgrounds (Casey and Koshy, 2013).

During the era of NAGTY, the government provided schools with resources to identify and meet the needs of gifted and talented learners. All schools had GATCOs, although in some cases the roles were given to newly or recently qualified teachers as it was perceived to be a relatively easy area of responsibility. NAGTY was contracted to provide for the top 5% of all learners, but this presented an identification challenge. Was this the top 5% of the national cohort or the top 5% in each school? In practice, it became the top 5% in each school, which arguably disadvantaged learners in more selective schools as there were a greater number of bright learners. Although it was not government policy, many schools chose to cast the net wide at around 10%–15% to compensate for this. Transition from primary school to secondary school was also challenging, since the changing profile of learners meant that some students who may have been the brightest in their primary school were nowhere near the top 15% in secondary school. As a result, some were taken off the gifted and talented register and considered themselves to have been 'de-gifted'.

Summer schools were a core element of the NAGTY offer and they were popular amongst the gifted students. For some it was about the higher-level subject content, which was often provided by university academics. For others, it provided an opportunity to break down feelings of isolation and to be with others like themselves. It was noticeable in the summer schools that a significant proportion of learners had SEND needs and were hence learners with DME.

A range of other government-funded programmes encouraged schools to identify their most able learners. For example, Regional Partnerships were created to give a focus to locally based gifted and talented initiatives and these were highly successful with relatively little government support. The Dux Awards recognised the top performing Year 9 student in every secondary school in England via teacher nomination. This scheme then brought these students together for a day of enrichment and challenge. Similarly, local authorities used government funding to run local programmes for gifted and talented learners and to bring together networks of GATCOs. However, opportunities to link SENCOs and GATCOs under the banner of inclusion were never realised at any significant scale.

The University of Warwick hosted NAGTY and subsequently launched and funded IGGY, a global educational social network for gifted teenagers. IGGY went some way towards building a Community of Practice for gifted and talented learners, but without an expansive face-to-face offer. However, it struggled to retain its priority status in schools as education policy began to shift.

In 2007, the government funding that had underpinned NAGTY was reassigned to CfBT (Centre for British Teachers) at a much-reduced level of funding and with a changed remit, which expanded to include primary schools. The perception from school leaders was that the focus had shifted away from provision and towards process, since the highest profile activity during this period was the collation of gifted and talented registers, but with limited accountability or purpose. Ultimately, a combination of sector incongruence and political changes (e.g. the disbanding of the National Strategies teams in 2011) led to the implosion of national policy and funding for gifted and talented provision in England. Local authorities and schools were expected to continue with gifted and talented initiatives using their own funding and absorbing the costs into their core provision. However, the lack of statutory accountability meant that by the end of 2011, most gifted and talented provision was lost at a local level and only a small number of Regional Partnerships remained.

In parallel to the changes in England, it is noteworthy that other parts of the UK have retained elements of High Learning Potential provision within their broader conceptions of inclusion. This is noticeable even within the language that is used to describe the equivalent role to SENCOs in England. For example, there are ALNCOs (Additional Learning Needs Co-ordinators) in Wales where 'additional learning needs' is interpreted as including appropriate provision for children with High Learning Potential. Broader still, Scotland uses the term 'additional support needs', which is understood to include any potential barrier to learning, even temporary needs, such as bullying or family issues (Education Scotland, 2019). In Northern Ireland, the intention is to introduce the role of Learning Support Co-ordinators (Purdy and Boddison, 2018).

In 2018, the British Government introduced plans to expand the number of grammar school places in England through a £50m selective schools expansion fund. Despite significant criticism, some grammar schools were given authority to grow, once again under the banner of social mobility (Abrams, 2019). Around the same time, the Future Talent Fund was launched, an £18m social mobility programme, but this ended up being shelved as the government instead focused its funding on early years provision (Whittaker, 2018).

When considering the successive challenges in targeting funding and education policy at those with High Learning Potential, it is clear that positioning DME squarely within the sphere of gifted and talented policy is problematic and highly influenced by the constant shifts in public opinion and political will. The fundamental principle of DME is that it rests in two domains; High Learning Potential and SEND. It is becoming increasingly clear that prioritising High Learning Potential within the SEND community is likely to be more strategically stable than prioritising SEND within the High Learning Potential community.

Since the introduction of the Children and Families Act 2014 and a revised SEND Code of Practice in January 2015, there has been a renewed focus on provision for those with Special Educational Needs. This set of SEND reforms has sought to place children and young people and their families at the centre, with the ambition that all learners with SEND reach their full potential. By definition, this includes learners with DME and so the opportunity to advocate for DME has arisen once again, but this time from the more politically stable perspective of those with High Learning Potential within the SEND community.

SEND provision is a growing national priority, which is increasingly in the spotlight because of the impact of school funding pressures and rising school exclusions. Similarly, the introduction of a new Education Inspection Framework (EIF) by Ofsted during 2019 has provided school leaders with the opportunity to think more about the appropriateness of their curriculum offer and there is a particular focus on learners with SEND. This is likely to bring DME to the fore once more, but the challenge will be in ensuring that the workforce is equipped to respond. Discussions about DME often begin with high-functioning learners with autism or with the High Learning Potential of those with physical disabilities. However, the broader notions of SEND and High Learning Potential can be overlooked and this is arguably a key area for workforce development.

In 2008, the Department for Education published 'Gifted and Talented Education: Helping to Find and Support Children with Dual or Multiple Exceptionalities' as part of the National Strategies programme (DfE, 2008). The focus of the publication was on tackling underachievement and many of the recommendations for schools in relation to effective provision are still relevant today, including:

- matching tasks to abilities and interests;
- allowing pupils with DME to share learning in ways that work for them;
- ensuring the classroom environment is appropriate in meeting their SEND;
- maintaining an appropriately paced lesson;
- following the child's interests;
- allowing non-standard responses to tasks;
- having high expectations;
- identifying learning strengths.

More recently, DME has appeared within a strand of work within the government's SEND Schools Workforce Contract, which was being delivered by nasen. Within this contract, a pilot programme of workforce development has been funded for Potential Plus UK to upskill teachers to be able to better identify and meet the needs of learners with DME. Similarly, DME was referenced within the Gatsby Good Career Guidance (Boddison, 2019) and it is once again starting to be discussed in different parts of the wider education system.

Box 2.1 An introduction to Kerry

Kerry is 8 years old and is one of three siblings. She attends a one-form entry maintained primary school and reports that she finds every single day a challenge. Kerry has a mature and academically advanced view of the world around her, but she doesn't understand why others can't see things the way that she does. She struggles to cope with her own emotional turbulence and is increasingly frustrated with other people.

Kerry's parents first noticed something wasn't right when she started school and they received contradictory progress reports. The reports showed the highest levels of attainment across all subject areas, but the effort grades were mixed. The school was increasingly contacting Kerry's parents about what they described as 'unacceptable behaviours' both in the classroom and in the playground. By the time Kerry was 7 years old, school life had become very hard for her. She had been excluded from social groups by the parents of her peers and was not invited to birthday parties, when the rest of her class were invited. The school were keeping her inside during break and lunch-times 'for the safety of other children' and they had warned Kerry's parents that she was at risk of school exclusion.

Kerry felt isolated by the position in which she found herself and the challenging behaviours, tantrums and violence started to happen at home as well as at school. When Kerry was angry or upset, she physically lashed out at her siblings and parents and she would grunt and growl; she kicked walls and furniture, slammed doors and stamped up the stairs. Very often, Kerry would hit herself repeatedly in the head when she was angry with herself and she would call herself stupid, blaming herself for not being able to control her emotions and behaviours.

Kerry's parents were not sure what to do and they became very concerned when Kerry started saying that she wished she was dead and that she wanted to kill herself. She repeatedly said that she hated herself and thought that everybody around her hated her too because of how she was behaving.

It was during these two years, that some of Kerry's talents, particularly in the creative arts, really become clear too, although it was not obvious to her parents at the time.

At school, Kerry had low levels of tolerance to other people being in her personal space and her response was generally violent. Rather than being sensitive to certain textures, Kerry seemed to crave them. For example, she was often found in school rubbing walls and railings, licking her cutlery and squeezing different fabrics in her hands.

Kerry's full story can be found in Chapter 5.

Understanding the workforce

Before implementing any form of workforce development, it is useful to understand the ideological demographic of the teachers and support staff. It is a reasonable assumption to think that most teachers joined the profession because they wanted to make a difference to children and young people, regardless of their current levels of attainment. Essentially, they want every child to be the best that they can be.

However, the reality is that some teachers will have a natural predisposition to want to work with some of the most vulnerable learners in our schools, such as those with SEND, those from disadvantaged backgrounds or looked-after children. The SENCO may be one such individual and with their team of support staff they are likely to know which other teachers in the school also share this predisposition. Similarly, some teachers will have a natural predisposition to want to work with high attaining learners or those with an avid interest in their particular subject area. Teachers who go above and beyond to ensure all learners are stretched and challenged will be included in this group, as well as those who provide extra-curricular activities focused on specific areas of interest or expertise. There will of course be those incredible teachers who can naturally do both and enjoy both, and these are ideal DME advocates or champions for the school.

Of course, the type of school and the demographic of the local population can have an impact here. For example, it is reasonable to assume that teachers in a special school have chosen to be there because they are mostly interested in supporting learners with SEND, whilst teachers in a grammar school have chosen to be there because they are mostly interested in those with High Learning Potential.

Understanding the balance of the ideological demographic across a school can help to decide on the best way to approach the development of the workforce. If the balance is tipped more towards supporting learners with SEND, then any strategy should focus on recognising that these learners may have an exceptional level of potential and that they should try to maximise it. Conversely, if the balance is tipped more towards supporting those with High Learning Potential, then the strategy should be focused on meeting individual needs and removing barriers to learning. In a mixed environment, it could be useful to begin with both strategies and then move towards a consistent whole-school approach to DME. This would help to ensure that all staff could see how effective provision for learners with DME is aligned to their own values-base.

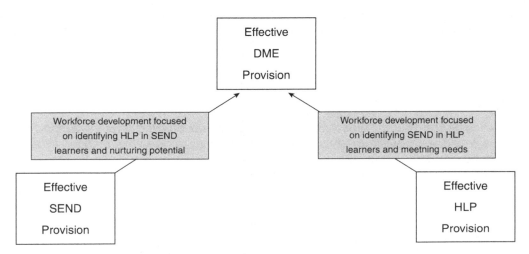

Figure 2.2 DME workforce development.

Making the case for change

In order to make the case for change and to secure buy-in from the wider workforce, it is useful to establish what is already happening that may be supporting the identification and meeting of needs for learners with DME. It is clear from the 'DME: The Current State of Play' report commissioned by nasen (Ryan and Waterman, 2018), that most education professionals in most schools are unaware of the concept of DME. Therefore, making the case for an awareness campaign should be a minimum expectation for the vast majority of schools, but, in looking beyond this, there are some simple indicators that can provide an immediate insight. For example, school leaders in England could reasonably expect a SENCO to know which students with EHC (Education, Health and Care) plans or on SEN Support also have High Learning Potential. Similarly, the GATCO could reasonably expect to know who the learners with SEND are that would benefit from HLP provision.

From a practical perspective, it would be good to understand whether the SENCO and the GATCO are comparing the lists of children on the SEND register with those on the Gifted and Talented Register. Given the expected prevalence of DME identified in Chapter 1, most schools could reasonably expect to have one to two learners with DME in an average class of 30 pupils. So, if this comparison of SEND and HLP registers has no overlap, it may be an indicator that the accuracy and quality of identification needs to be further developed. If the registers do overlap, it would be a useful exercise to understand what the school offer looks like for these learners and to assess the extent to which that offer is effective, scalable, replicable and sustainable.

Some schools have chosen to appoint to roles focused on a broader notion of inclusion, such as *Head of Inclusion* or *Inclusion Co-ordinator*. In most cases, this seems to broaden the remit of the role beyond SEND to include other vulnerable groups such as looked-after children and those from disadvantaged backgrounds. It is less common for this to also include children and young people with High Learning Potential, but it is certainly possible to put forward a compelling argument that it should. In Scotland and Wales, the inclusion of High Learning Potential within the remit of inclusion-focused positions may be more prevalent, since they do not use the term Special Educational Needs. Instead, Scotland and Wales use the terms *additional support needs* and *additional learning needs* respectively.

It is quite common for skills audits to be used by boards of governors or trustees to inform recruitment and training needs. This approach is less common within the school workforce, but for specialist and targeted areas like DME, it can be a useful approach. When undertaking a general staff survey, some additional questions could be included to assess the knowledge, confidence and skills of staff in relation to DME and any relevant training that has been undertaken. Not only can this inform the approach to workforce development, it can also be repeated at a later stage to measure the impact across these key domains.

Similarly, it can be a useful exercise to ask parents and carers to share what they think are the key areas of High Learning Potential for their own children and to reflect on what the school's offer is in that context. This approach does come with somewhat of a health warning in that some parents and carers could have biased views, which under- or overestimate their child's potential. Nevertheless, parents and carers do have a unique insight into their own children and often know them better than anybody else, so they are well placed to identify unfulfilled potential.

Box 2.2 An introduction to Jack

From when he first started nursery, Jack's behaviour has been difficult for the school to deal with. He would stand still and scream, making it very hard to divert his attention away from any task he wanted to undertake.

Jack had low social awareness and interaction with peers. Instead, he talked to adults as equals and on occasion tried to demand their attention regardless of the time or place. It was also difficult to gauge Jack's true ability as he frequently refused to complete tasks without one-to-one support. Whilst still at nursery, Jack was put on the SEND register for behaviour support and strategies.

After a difficult time at nursery, Jack continued to display challenging behaviour at the start of primary school. However, Jack was imaginative, loved playing board-games and learning facts, and he had a boundless passion for mathematics. Jack's parents recognised that they needed to have a better understanding of his areas of strength, as they didn't want all the focus to be only on his difficulties at the expense of other things.

Jack's full story can be found in Chapter 5.

Better identification

The nuances and specifics of identification and assessment for individual Special Educational Needs, such as dyslexia or autism, are not covered in this book as they are well documented elsewhere. Similarly, this book will not delve into IQ testing or cognitive ability tests as approaches for identifying High Learning Potential. There are also commercial packages of published software available that support schools with effective assessments. However, this book will consider how a combination of formal and informal identified needs, including High Learning Potential, can be used to make a case for identifying DME.

Given that both SEND and High Learning Potential are complex in their own right, it is perhaps unsurprising that the identification of DME has a high level of complexity. Identification is not an exact science and we would echo the advice of Professor Diane Montgomery in relation to adopting a triangulation approach (Montgomery, 2015). Triangulation in this context refers to indicators and identifiers of SEND and High Learning Potential that may come from a broad range of sources. The concept is that teachers look to identify multiple indicators of DME (a minimum of three, depending upon the strength of evidence available). These indicators may be inconclusive in isolation, but together they begin to make a compelling case that the learner has DME.

For SEND, the indicators may include a formal identification of specific conditions by education psychologists. They might also include other forms of identification such as family identification, or identification based on classroom observation, parental concerns or the use of diagnostic assessment software. For High Learning Potential, this might be, for example,

IQ tests, CAT tests, teacher observation (flashes of brilliance) or even self-identification. Regardless of the specific identification methods, the principle of triangulation here is that the more indicators of SEND and HLP there are, the more likely it is that the learner has DME.

To get a sense of how this might work in practice, below are four examples of evidence where serious consideration should be given to an identification of DME. These examples are focused on the identification of DME, rather than provision, but this is covered throughout the book.

Table 2.1

Example 1	Example 2
• Year 10 pupil (age 14) • IQ test score of 136 • In bottom set for GCSE English • Highly knowledgeable about Pokémon • Excellent chess player • Reading age of 11	• Year 8 pupil (age 12) • Has had 3 fixed term exclusions • Maths report says he is an excellent problem-solver, but maths test results are often 30–40% • On SEND register for social, emotional and mental health needs • Parents are confused as they say he is good at maths. He does the accounts for the family business
Example 3	**Example 4**
• Year 4 pupil (age 8) • Visual impairment – requires enlarged text and/or use of a laptop in lessons • Average attainment in all subject areas with dedicated one-to-one support from a teaching assistant • Grade 8 musician in multiple instruments including violin, piano and clarinet	• Foundation Stage pupil (age 5) • Underperformance against all Early Years Foundation Stage development targets (12 months behind) • Parents do not want child on the SEND register because they do not want the label, but the SENCO thinks he needs support • Class teacher believes the child could fly with the right support, but this has been difficult as the child rarely speaks • An educational psychologist who was actually observing a different pupil has inadvertently noted flashes of excellence with this child that have been missed by teachers and parents, including the ordering of cars according to the rainbow spectrum and the ability to tell the time on an analogue clock

In taking this triangulation approach to DME, there is a greater than average chance of overidentification. Given this potential for overidentification, it is reasonable to consider what the risk would be if an individual was identified with DME when they did not truly fit a DME profile. The basic premise of DME provision is that SEND needs will be identified and met and High Learning Potential will be identified and nurtured. Therefore, it could be argued that effective provision for learners with DME is not dissimilar to effective provision for all learners.

On this basis, a learner with some DME traits receiving provision designed for a learner with a fuller DME profile is unlikely to suffer any significant negative consequences as a result. Conversely, the risk of failing to identify a learner with DME is much greater. If the SEND needs are unmet or the level of challenge is pitched inappropriately, the learner could get bored or become disaffected. In some cases, this could lead to challenging behaviours, increased anxiety or school exclusion. Therefore, it is better to be inclusive and to cast the net wide to maximise the chances that all learners with DME are identified rather than take an exclusive approach, which risks excluding some individuals.

The indicators of SEND or High Learning Potential may not always be obvious in a classroom setting as some learners with DME use advanced coping strategies, which have the effect of masking both the needs and the potential. It is therefore useful for the wider workforce to have some understanding of DME too, so that they can be alert to any indicators, both within and beyond the classroom, that could support identification through triangulation.

• **Example 1** – it may be a lunchtime supervisor in the school playground who notices a child struggling with co-ordination and movement, which may not be so easy to notice in a classroom setting. When this information is considered alongside the teacher identifying that the child is excelling in mathematics and the parents sharing that the child is devouring advanced books at home, then a triangulated identification of DME begins to emerge. In this case, it may be that there is dyspraxia coupled with academic excellence.

- **Example 2** – imagine a child who has average progress and attainment in class, but every now and then there are flashes of brilliance. This might be an answer to a question in the classroom that shows advanced understanding or a unique insight into a particular concept. However and whenever this occurs, it should be noted down. In this example, it may be that the learner has dyslexia or some other form of literacy difficulties and this is hampering them from showing the same brilliance in their written work as they can in their oral work. The learner could be working incredibly hard and at an advanced level to overcome the particular literacy difficulties, but the outcome is an average written performance where the difficulties become masked and the potential is not realised. This is an example of coping strategies being used, which can be exhausting for learners and could impact on their anxiety levels if used over an extended period of time.
- **Example 3** – consider a learner who is struggling in school with maths and English. In order to support the learner, the school has provided booster lessons in maths and English, which take place when the rest of the class are doing PE and sports. As a consequence, the school may be unaware that the learner has exceptional athletic and sporting abilities. Using the triangulation approach and working closely with the family, this information is more likely to be shared and it can then be factored into a potential identification of DME.

In order to use the triangulation approach, there does need to be some form of centralised recording/monitoring system. As far as possible, this should be based on systems that are already in place within the school and with which it is easy for staff to engage. Many schools now use CRM (Customer Relationship Management) systems to keep a record of accidents, meetings with parents and academic performance, amongst other things. This could easily be extended to facilitate identification through triangulation in a way that is built-in rather than being a bolt-on.

As can be seen from the examples discussed in this chapter, a central premise of the effective identification of DME is meaningful engagement with families and learner-centred provision. Multidisciplinary collaboration (e.g. across education, health and social care) and coproduction of provision are both driving principles of the Children and Families Act 2014. These principles are very much applicable to DME, since, in addition to being a subset of HLP, DME is also a subset of SEND. In considering how well equipped the workforce may be to identify DME, it is useful to consider the extent to which coproduction and meaningful engagement with families is happening. Some key reflection questions to consider are:

- What regular opportunities are there for staff in our school to have meaningful, child-centred discussions with families?
- How do learners share their aspirations, achievements and successes?
- What is our approach to balancing external curriculum expectations with the individual needs and learning potential of our pupils?

Another reason that identification through triangulation is a good approach is because it reinforces the idea that identifying and meeting needs is everybody's responsibility. There is always a risk that if something is everybody's responsibility, then everybody thinks everybody else is doing it, so they personally do not need to. We need to get to a position where DME genuinely is everybody's responsibility, much like the way in which safeguarding is viewed in schools. Around ten to 15 years ago, the idea of safeguarding being everybody's responsibility sometimes meant that everybody thought everybody else was doing it and so in practice nobody took responsibility. That has now changed in schools and in addition to safeguarding leads, there is a genuine sense of everybody taking their responsibility seriously. This journey towards meaningful corporate responsibility for DME is where schools need to get to and the journey to get to this point is as important as the destination itself. The SEND Code of Practice 2015 contains the concept that every teacher is a teacher of learners with SEND. By extension, we need to be in a position where every teacher is a teacher of learners with DME.

An interesting and often overlooked dimension of DME is the capacity for self-identification. The higher-level cognitive capacity of some learners with DME means that they may be very aware of their own High Learning Potential and their own individual needs, as well as having a unique insight into what teaching and learning strategies will be most effective for them. In developing the workforce, it is important to think about how school staff can become more open to conversations with pupils that encourage them to be more reflective learners.

With the wider workforce contributing to the identification of DME, there does then need to be a central person co-ordinating things. Ideally, this should be the SENCO, the GATCO or the person responsible for inclusion because they are in a position to quality assure the evidence base being used for the triangulation and they can secure external expertise as required, such as educational psychologists, occupational therapists or speech and language therapists. As the SENCO has a statutory responsibility for co-ordinating SEND provision, it makes sense that the SENCO or Head of Inclusion should oversee DME provision with input from the GATCO and others as required.

Better provision

Once the workforce is better equipped to identify DME, the obvious next step is to ensure that they are better equipped to put effective provision in place for learners with DME. A concern that teachers may have in relation to provision is that this is yet another thing for them to do within the context of an already packed and ever-expanding schedule. It is therefore important to emphasise the point made earlier in this chapter that the focus should be about building as much into existing provision as possible rather than bolting on additional provision. The latter is unsustainable and can often be prohibitive in terms of time and money.

The two key elements of effective DME provision are meeting individual needs and nurturing High Learning Potential. Most schools already have well-established systems in place for meeting individual needs and there is no reason that learners with DME provision cannot access these core services. However, some of the content may need to be adapted to ensure it is appropriate.

For example, let us consider a pupil with literacy difficulties who is struggling with a comprehension exercise in an English lesson. One approach might be to provide a simpler text for the pupil so that they can access an easier comprehension exercise. However, this may not be an appropriate form of differentiation if the pupil has High Learning Potential, since it was the process of reading the text that was challenging rather than the level of the content. In this situation, a more appropriate form of differentiation could be the use of assistive technology that converts text to speech as this would have removed the barrier to learning without removing access to the higher-level cognitive content.

In relation to nurturing High Learning Potential, an important concept to remember is that every learner deserves a challenge. Jason Buckley is the Director of Studies at *GIFT*, an organisation that provides workshops and residential courses for gifted children in the UK. He often discusses the concepts of 'equality of challenge' and 'equality of struggle', both of which have significant relevance for learners with DME. A mistake sometimes made by teachers when setting extension work is to give 'more of the same work' rather than 'more challenging work'. As part of a workforce development programme, it is useful for teachers to have time to think through the features of more challenging work and to ensure that learners can use appropriate higher-order thinking skills and that they have access to a strengths-based curriculum.

It can be a useful exercise to reflect regularly on the equality of challenge provided to learners with DME. This can be achieved in several ways, such as ensuring this is built into lesson observation criteria or using a reflective tool for teaching and learning, such as lesson study. Lesson study is a collaborative model of professional development where the learning of individual pupils is observed instead of focusing on the teacher. The effectiveness of this approach has been assessed by the Education Endowment Foundation and the Teacher Development Trust and it is generally thought to be an effective tool (Ming Cheung and Yee Wong, 2014; Godfrey et al., 2017).

A key element of workforce development is to consider the role of the teacher sometimes as a facilitator rather than as an expert. The reality is that, in some circumstances, a pupil with High Learning Potential could very quickly advance beyond the knowledge and experience of the teacher. In such situations, the teacher may feel vulnerable or inadequate, but they need not be overly concerned as this situation presents an opportunity to allow the learner to shine. The teacher is well placed to signpost the learner towards resources, experts and activities that will nurture their talents. During teacher training days, time could be given to teachers to work collaboratively to identify an appropriate set of extension resources for each individual learner with DME.

Summary

The key stages of equipping the school workforce are: understanding the national policy context, understanding the workforce, making the case for change, better identification and better provision. It can be useful for the SENCO to lead on workforce development if DME is a subset of SEND but, as discussed earlier, the GATCO or Director of Inclusion must be involved and, in some circumstances, they may lead the process themselves. However, SENCOs should be mindful that learners with DME and their families may not wish to be identified as having SEND due to wider societal preconceptions and may prefer instead to be formally associated with the High Learning Potential aspect of DME. Similarly, there will be some who take the view that labels are for bottles, not learners, and such views should always be respected.

At a national level, consideration ought to be given for DME to have its own status that draws from both SEND and High Learning Potential. Ultimately, SENCOs should recognise that effective DME provision is about personalised learning and inclusion and it is not easy to achieve without input from a broad range of key stakeholders.

For identification, triangulation is a sensible approach and this involves meaningful engagement with families as well as a learner-centred culture. The two key outcomes of equipping the workforce in relation to DME are better identification and better provision, which lead to individual needs being more effectively met and High Learning Potential being more effectively nurtured.

Box 2.3 Ten myths of supporting pupils with DME

Myth No. 3: Pupils cannot have HLP and lack basic skills; it just means they are lazy or aren't trying.

It can be difficult to believe that a child or young person who has so much knowledge or who is extremely talented can have issues with things like reading or writing or spelling. However, students with DME will show uneven levels of ability (sometimes known as a 'spiky profile') and can struggle with the most basic of activities such as the speed or legibility of their handwriting; skills which their classmates often master long before they do.

Myth No. 4: How can more able pupils struggle so much with their working memory or processing speed; are they just not listening?

Many children with DME have issues with their executive functioning skills; such as working memory, processing speed and organisational skills. It is not that they are deliberately misbehaving in class, it is just that they genuinely struggle to compensate for these difficulties. There are some simple things which teachers and others can do which may benefit others in the class such as always giving pupils time to process questions before then asking for answers. Some schools used the 'flipped classroom' approach, in which pupils are given questions to consider in advance of the lesson and these are then explored during the lesson itself.

3   Leadership and governance

I became a school governor to help other parents with children with DME to get the support they need. However, it is really difficult to make the case for DME when I see the lack of resources the school has and the conflicting pressures on them. However, surely children with DME also deserve support?

(Parent governor)

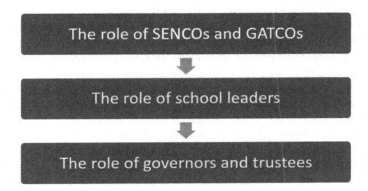

Figure 3.1

Effective school leadership is a cornerstone of ensuring that the needs of all learners are met so that they have the best chance of reaching their full potential. This chapter explores the role of SENCOs, GATCOs, school leaders, governors and trustees in creating an inclusive culture that maximises outcomes for learners with DME. There will be a specific focus on the use of data to review and inform provision as well as a discussion on how existing accountability processes can be adapted and developed to accommodate DME. The governance strategies shared are useful for all governance professionals, but will have a particular relevance for SEND governors, chairs and trustees of multi-academy trusts.

The role of SENCOs and GATCOs

The role of the SENCO is of critical importance in schools and this is recognised within national policy and legislation. To illustrate this point, it is noteworthy that only two roles are legally required in a school, the SENCO and the Headteacher; and, of these two roles, only the SENCO is required to be a qualified teacher. For more than 15 years, it has also been a requirement for SENCOs to achieve the National Award in Special Educational Needs Co-ordination, which is a Masters-level qualification.

The SEND Code of Practice 2015 is clear that every school must have a named SENCO and a key question is what role they should have in relation to the co-ordination of DME provision. As discussed in Chapter 2, it should be the SENCO, GATCO or Director of Inclusion that has the oversight of workforce development and responsibility for co-ordinating the identification of and provision for learners with DME. The important word here is 'co-ordination' since SENCOs and GATCOs should be building capacity in the wider workforce rather than doing it all themselves. Ideally, the SENCO and/or GATCO should be a member of staff who has significant expertise and experience in terms of DME and if they are not already aware of DME, it would be good for school leaders to encourage and support them to develop their knowledge base in this important area.

The SEND Code of Practice 2015 states that SENCOs should be on the senior leadership team in schools and this is an example of where their expertise in DME can have a significant impact. When strategic decisions are made by the senior leadership team, having the SENCO in the room is essential since they can use their expertise to ensure that any potential impact on learners with DME has been properly considered. The SENCO is well placed to ask the right questions at the point that decisions are being made rather than having to pick up any pieces afterwards due to the unintended consequences of bad decisions made in good faith.

When the SEND Code of Practice 2015 was being drawn up, there was significant debate about whether the statutory guidance ought to state that SENCOs *should* be on the senior leadership team or *must* be on the senior leadership team. One of the criticisms of *must* was a fear that SENCOs would be drawn away from the SENCO role to undertake wider leadership responsibilities such as bus duty, gate duty and withdrawing learners from classrooms in response to challenging behaviour. Ultimately, the inclusion of *should* in the final published document means that whilst SENCOs should be on the senior leadership team, school leaders can choose not to do this. In such circumstances, it is important that there is an appropriate mechanism in place to ensure that SENCOs can have an influence on strategic decision-making. If this is not done, there is a significant risk of decisions being made that have unintended consequences for learners with DME.

School leaders should think carefully about how SENCOs are using their time. In too many schools, SENCOs are spending vast amounts of time collating paperwork, despite being one of the most well-qualified education professionals. If the SENCO in your school is spending more time on paperwork and completing administrative tasks than on improving teaching and learning, then this is a very expensive administrator. One of the recommendations of the National SENCO Workload Survey (Curran et al., 2018) is to invest in the team around the SENCO. For example, it may be worth ensuring that the SENCO has access to dedicated administrative support or an Assistant SENCO to ensure that they can focus on strategic issues and on improving teaching and learning. The premise of the Workload Survey was about assessing whether or not SENCOs have enough protected time to discharge their duties. As a school leader or a governor, you should be confident that your SENCO has sufficient protected time to co-ordinate provision for learners with DME. This is an important point, since in many schools this pool of learners is likely to be broader than expected.

In relation to DME, a key responsibility for the SENCO is to ensure that there is collaboration with the GATCO. When there is meaningful and effective communication between the SENCO and the GATCO, the identification and associated provision for learners with DME has the best chance of being impactful in a positive sense. As the two professionals with responsibility for SEND and High Learning Potential respectively, the SENCO and the GATCO are arguably the lynchpins of provision for learners with DME. Some schools choose to merge these roles together in the form of a Director of Inclusion and, if implemented correctly, this can be a powerful way of ensuring that DME is a key strategic priority.

A potential strategy to support a child with DME in school

- Senior leadership team and board of governors or trustees agree to adopt a school-wide policy of supporting DME.
- A DME lead governor or trustee is appointed and DME is added to policy documents along with SEND and gifted and talented (or equivalent).
- The SENCO and GATCO develop a joint programme to support all the needs of learners with DME.
- Individual provision maps or EHC plans are in place and available to support the Special Educational Needs of learners with DME and to nurture their talent.
- A strengths-based approach is supported, developed and implemented.
- Families are involved and supported to develop a plan to support learning at home. There will be a common understanding of how issues in school will be handled where the learner with DME may have particular difficulties such as exams, project work, writing or homework.
- Information and/or training will be provided to all relevant class and subject teachers to encourage a flexible strengths-based approach to learning. For example, if handwriting is

an issue for the child, the teacher will consider other ways for them to record what they have learnt (e.g. PowerPoint) or for the use of assistive technology (e.g. speech to text programmes).
- Success is celebrated by focusing on what the learner can do rather than what they cannot do.

Another aspect of the SENCO or GATCO role is the liaison with other providers, external agencies and educational psychologists and all of these can be crucial steps in securing appropriate provision for learners with DME. In addition to securing specialist input to meet the individual needs of learners, it is important that SENCOs are content with the provision that has been put in place to maximise High Learning Potential. Conversely, GATCOs ought to be content with the provision that has been put in place in relation to SEND.

It is worth making the point here that some education professionals have been known to express concern that maximising High Learning Potential for learners with DME could be seen as elitist or exclusive. However, there is a robust challenge to this view on the basis that learners with DME are by definition a vulnerable group within our education system, since they have SEND. More directly, there is the argument that meeting the needs of pupils with High Learning Potential is not indifferent to meeting the needs of learners with SEND, since they are both about removing individual barriers to learning. Meeting the needs of learners with DME is simply inclusive practice.

The SEN Information Report is a statutory document that every school in England has been required to publish on their school website since 2014. The expectation is that schools will review the SEN Information Report annually and ensure it is updated. This report is intended to be a live document that gives schools the chance to celebrate their inclusive practice, including their provision for learners with DME. As a SENCO, it would be useful to reflect on the extent to which the SEN Information Report sets out for families the details of DME provision within the school.

SENCOs will already be familiar with the four broad areas of need as set out in the SEND Code of Practice 2015 and GATCOs should ensure that they too are familiar with them:

- communication and interaction;
- cognition and learning;
- social, emotional and mental health;
- sensory and/or physical needs.

Paragraph 6.30 within the Code of Practice provides a further explanation of the broad area of cognition and learning:

> 'Support for learning difficulties may be required when children and young people learn at a slower pace than their peers, even with appropriate differentiation.'
>
> (DfE and DoH, 2015, p. 97)

When considering High Learning Potential, it could be argued that these children and young people generally learn at a faster pace than their peers, but this is not always the case. The two key words here are potential and differentiation. There is the potential for children with DME to learn at a faster pace than their peers, but appropriate differentiation must be put in place, not only to meet their needs, but also to nurture their learning potential.

Removing barriers to learning is only part of the required provision for learners with DME, since it is essential to also follow the child's interests. This aligns to a key principle of the Children and Families Act 2014, which promotes learner-centred provision. DME provision that removes barriers to learning but does not follow the child's interests, may result in learning that is still at a slower pace than their peers as the potential may not be realised. The door will be open, but there may be no motivation to go through it.

Returning to the explanation of cognition and learning needs, children with DME may be characterised as learning at a significantly faster and/or slower pace than their peers dependent on the provision that has been put in place. It is therefore appropriate for SENCOs to encourage teachers to be on the lookout for significant changes in the pace of learning as one potential indicator of DME. Teachers have sometimes described this constant shifting in learning pace as 'average with flashes of brilliance'. SENCOs who have the characteristics of DME in mind when identifying cognition and learning needs will have an increased chance of being more effective when co-ordinating appropriate provision.

Box 3.1 An introduction to Jamie

Jamie stopped going to school when he was 10 years old because of a variety of different issues including Autism Spectrum Condition and Emotional and Behavioural Difficulties (EBD). The home tuition service of the local authority had been trying to engage him in education and had been sending tutors into his home for over three years. However, there had been little success with this and over the years Jamie had developed low confidence and self-esteem, severe anxiety, social phobia and finally agoraphobia. All of this meant that Jamie did not leave his bedroom and had become an elective mute. This made educating him extremely difficult, even though he was seen as a bright boy.

Engaging with Jamie and providing him with a worthwhile education had become extremely complicated. He would knock on his bedroom door to communicate; once for yes and twice for no. He would also pass messages under the door but would have no face-to-face interaction with the tutors sent in to provide his education. This was worrying and of concern to everyone involved.

Jamie's full story can be found in Chapter 5.

The role of school leaders

In schools where provision for learners with DME is most effective, there is often a strong leadership focus on inclusion. It can be more challenging if a school leader takes the approach that they will run the school, whilst the SENCO looks after inclusion – this is not real inclusion. The most inclusive schools ensure that strategic decision-making is always done through the lens of inclusion. For example, decisions made about curriculum design or about teaching and learning more broadly should be made so that they work for all learners from the outset rather than having to be adapted retrospectively for some learners. This 'built-in not bolt-on' approach to school leadership can be empowering in supporting teachers to identify and meet the needs of learners with DME.

In order to be an effective leader of DME, it is important to create a culture where excellence and equity go hand in hand. In music, sports, drama and art, there is an expectation that talent and High Learning Potential are identified and nurtured so that individuals can excel. However, when the potential is more academic, there can be less consistency, with decisions on provision sometimes based more on the wider profile of needs than on those of the individual.

For example, there is an accountability expectation that all children should reach a minimum standard in mathematics and English, so resources tend to focus on maximising the number of learners that meet this minimum threshold. Given that resources are finite, there is a trade-off between this expectation and resourcing provision for those with High Learning Potential who could significantly exceed this level. In sports, art, music and drama there are fewer statutory expectations around minimum levels of competency, so the focus is instead on engagement, developing a passion for the subject and a significant push for those with High Learning Potential.

Some subjects lend themselves to a low-threshold, high-ceiling approach, which is where all children can access a subject, but those with High Learning Potential have the opportunity to excel (differentiation by outcome). School leaders should foster a culture where there is an equity across the curriculum in relation to both accessibility and excellence, as this is an environment in which learners with DME can thrive. Children who have the potential to excel in academic subjects deserve to have that potential realised as much as those who have the potential to excel in music, sports, drama or art.

When school leaders are considering their strategic approach to identifying and meeting the Special Educational Needs of learners, the use of publicly available datasets can be a useful starting point. Every school in England has a statutory duty to complete the school census[1] and this includes providing information about the profile of Special Educational Needs in the school. Every summer, the Department for Education publishes 'Special Educational Needs in England',[2] which is a summary of the data collected in January of the same year. Within these statistics is the proportion of learners by primary area of need at both national and local authority level. It is a useful exercise to compare the data for your own school or group of schools against the local and national data. It is not about conforming to local or national averages, but where there are differences, it is good to understand why and to ensure that resources are aligned to the school's profile of needs.

Example

To get an idea of how this might work in practice, here is an example of how a fictitious school from Blackpool, Lady Videtta High School, might use the census data from January 2019.

Table 3.1

	Specific Learning Difficulty	Moderate Learning Difficulty	Severe Learning Difficulty	Profound & Multiple Learning Difficulty	Social, Emotional and Mental Health	Speech, Language and Communications Needs	Hearing Impairment	Visual Impairment	Multisensory Impairment	Physical Disability	Autistic Spectrum Disorder	Other Difficulty/Disability	SEN support but no Specialist assessment of type of need	Total
	\multicolumn{14}{c}{*Proportion of Learners by Primary Area of Need (%)*}													
Lady Videtta High School	4.7	29.5	0.0	0.0	25.7	23.8	1.3	1.2	0.8	0.3	2.9	4.1	5.7	100
Blackpool	5.6	23.2	0.3	0.0	21.0	39.0	1.3	1.1	0.8	2.7	3.2	1.4	0.4	100
England	9.5	20.9	0.6	0.3	16.3	30.6	1.7	0.9	0.3	2.8	7.9	3.9	4.3	100

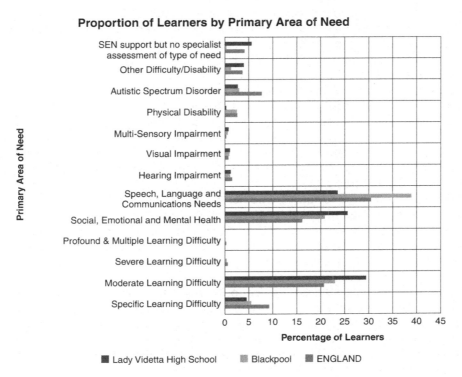

Figure 3.2 Analysis by primary area of need.

A school leader at Lady Videtta High School analysing this data might consider the following:

1. The proportion of learners with SEN Support but no Specialist Assessment of Type of Need at Lady Videtta High School is higher than national and significantly higher than for Blackpool. A similar pattern occurs for Other Difficulty/Disability. For Moderate Learning Difficulty, the proportion is significantly higher at Lady Videtta High School than both Blackpool and England. These three areas of need are similar in that they are broad 'catch-all' type categories. This suggests that accurate identification of needs may be an issue at Lady Videtta High School and this should be explored further. It is also notable that the proportion of learners with Speech, Language and Communication Needs is lower than both Blackpool and England. Could it be that some of those learners with a broader identification of SEND have unidentified Speech, Language and Communication Needs? Do the processes for identifying these needs have an appropriate level of validity and reliability and specialist input?

2. The proportion of learners with Social, Emotional and Mental Health needs is higher at Lady Videtta High School than Blackpool and England. What provision does the school have in place to support well-being and what does this data suggest about the effectiveness of this provision? Is the school confident that unidentified, and therefore unmet, needs are not becoming anxiety issues over time? Are there any particular groups of learners who are most at risk of developing Social, Emotional and Mental Health difficulties and are school resources aligned to addressing this?

3. The proportion of learners with Autism Spectrum Disorder is in line with local data, but significantly below national data. Why might the patterns of identification in Blackpool vary so much from the national proportions? From a positive perspective, it may be that autism provision at Lady Videtta High School (and in Blackpool more broadly) is highly effective, with many learners having their needs met and therefore not being recorded as having SEND on the census.

    From a more challenging perspective, it may be that families in the local area do not have confidence in the autism provision offered and are choosing either to home school or to look at schools outside the local area. Does the school have an inclusive reputation? Is the school accessible and meeting its equalities obligations? How confident is the school that exclusion at the point of admission is not happening (e.g. 'there is a school up the road that would be much better able to meet the needs of your child')?

These lines of inquiry should help school leaders at Lady Videtta High School to better understand where barriers to inclusion may exist and can lead to a more effective deployment of the SENCO, GATCO or Director of Inclusion. The school leader may wish to work in partnership with the SEND governor and the SENCO to explore the answers to these questions and to build an evidence base, which can inform strategic decision-making.

A consistency issue that regularly arises is the process for determining the criteria for inclusion on the SEN register. Some schools take the view that a learner is only added to the register if they require provision that is different from or additional to that which is normally provided for all learners. Others will take the view that learners with formally identified needs should always be recorded even if those needs are already being met by high-quality teaching. School leaders should put measures in place to ensure that there is consistency within their school and they should liaise with other school leaders and the local authority to ensure that there is also consistency at a local level. This will increase the validity and reliability of the census data, particularly at the level of SEN Support.

School leaders who are reviewing whether the culture of their school is inclusive and assessing how effective it is for learners with DME should undertake an analysis of children who have left the school in the previous five years. Ofsted has become increasingly interested in understanding the reasons why children are leaving schools and their 'Education Inspection Framework' (Ofsted, 2019) includes a specific remit to hold school leaders to account for exclusions and off-rolling.

If learners are leaving because the school is unable to meet their needs, either SEND or High Learning Potential, then it will be important to understand how a different school has been able to meet their needs. Reflecting on this may be useful in establishing alternative approaches that support greater inclusion. Some families choose to remove their children from the school system altogether by opting for elective home education. At the time of writing, there is no public dataset that records rates of elective home education, but various freedom of information requests have shown significant increases over the past decade (Williams, 2018; Tuffin, 2019), with the

Children's Commissioner describing the number of children not educated in school as having 'rocketed' (Longfield, 2019). There are plans for a register of all children not educated in schools in England but, in the meantime, school leaders need to be confident that elective home education for students leaving their schools is a genuine pedagogical or lifestyle choice and is not because families feel it is their only option or a last resort.

There are numerous self-review, peer review and professional review tools that can support schools to identify strategic priorities in relation to SEND provision and High Learning Potential provision. For SEND, the freely available Whole School SEND review (Bartram and Patel, 2015) provides a framework for exploring eight key areas of focus:

- outcomes for pupils with SEND;
- leadership of SEND;
- the quality of teaching and learning for pupils with SEND;
- working with pupils and parents/carers of pupils with SEND;
- assessment and identification;
- monitoring, tracking and evaluation;
- the efficient use of resources;
- the quality of SEND provision.

For High Learning Potential, the freely available' National Quality Standards in Gifted and Talented Education' (Mouchel, 2005) provide a framework for exploring 14 key areas of focus across five broad areas:

- Effective teaching and learning strategies:
  - identification;
  - effective provision in the classroom;
  - standards.
- Enabling curriculum entitlement and choice:
  - enabling curriculum entitlement and choice.
- Assessment for learning:
  - assessment for learning;
  - transfer and transition.
- School organisation:
  - leadership;
  - policy;
  - school ethos and pastoral care;
  - staff development;
  - resources;
  - monitoring and evaluation.
- Strong partnership beyond the school:
  - engaging with the community, families and beyond;
  - learning beyond the classroom.

Whilst these tools are useful in their own right, using them in a targeted way for DME can be powerful. It can be enlightening to apply the SEND review tool with a specific focus on children with High Learning Potential. Similarly, it can be enlightening to apply the National Quality Standards in Gifted and Talented Education with a specific focus on learners with SEND. If multiple assessment tools are being used in this way, the following summary template may be a useful format for bringing together the findings into one document as the basis of an action plan.

Those looking for an existing off-the-shelf framework for inclusion more broadly, which includes HLP, SEND and DME may wish to consider the well-respected Inclusion Quality Mark.[3] Other HLP-focused frameworks include Nace's Challenge Award[4] and Potential Plus UK's High Learning Potential Best Practice Award.[5]

In 2008, the Department for Education published Gifted and Talented Education: Helping to Find and Support Children with Dual or Multiple Exceptionalities (DfE, 2008). Appendices 2 and 3 of this publication provide some useful DME self-assessment questions and provision descriptors that can be used by school leaders. A recurring theme in this publication and across all the tools for reviewing both SEND and High Learning Potential is leadership. Fundamentally, if there

Table 3.2

Area of Focus	HLP Findings	SEND Findings	Implications for Learners with DME	Actions
Leadership and Governance				
Identification				
Outcomes				
Quality of Teaching and Learning				
Quality of Coproduction				
Knowledge, Skills and Experience				
Other?				

is no leadership buy-in to DME as a school improvement priority, then effective DME provision will be very difficult to realise. It is school leaders who can set an inclusive culture in a school and this needs to come consistently from all leaders, including governors, trustees, senior leaders and middle leaders. If we want every teacher to be an effective teacher for learners with DME, then we need every leader to be a leader of DME.

As can be seen from the earlier discussion on elective home education, family confidence is an important indicator of an effective DME-friendly culture within a school or a MAT (multi-academy trust). However, workforce confidence (teachers and support staff) and leader confidence (governors/trustees and school leaders) are also both important indicators. As a simple starting point in establishing the level of confidence, each group might consider the following self-assessment questions. In each case, consideration should be given to the quality of evidence to support the judgements made.

Table 3.3

Leader Confidence	• Is the culture of the school inclusive and is there an ethos of supporting learners with DME? • Is there effective collaboration between the SENCO and the GATCO? • Do learners with DME achieve their potential? • Is there an identified strategy for DME within the school's development/improvement plan? • To what extent does teaching and learning routinely meet the needs of pupils with DME? • Do policies, processes and procedures reflect the views and expectations of learners with DME and their families?
Workforce Confidence	• Are teachers confident in identifying the SEND and High Learning Potential of pupils with DME? • Does professional development foster more effective provision for learners with DME? • Can the curriculum be implemented using a strengths-based approach that follows learners' individual interests? • Are support staff empowered to make an effective contribution to DME provision? • Is the balance of equity and excellence consistent and appropriate across all curriculum areas? • Are there clear roles and responsibilities in relation to DME?
Family Confidence	• Are learners with DME able to articulate how school provision meets their needs and nurtures their High Learning Potential? • Do learners feel equipped to self-identify DME? • Are there appropriate opportunities for enrichment and extra-curricular activities? • Is there genuine and meaningful coproduction in place for learners with DME and their families? • Are learners with DME appropriately prepared for adulthood? • Does the school assign value to a broader notion of outcomes beyond academic outcomes, as appropriate for learners with DME?

The role of governors and trustees

Some learners with DME achieve well in school since they develop effective coping strategies that allow them to overcome any unmet needs. However, there are too many learners with DME who under-achieve because they have insufficient opportunities to express and develop their High Learning Potential. Governors and trustees have a responsibility to ensure that there is effective provision in place for all learners, and this includes learners with DME. It is important to note that learners with DME are not a homogeneous group and what constitutes effective provision for one learner with DME may not be effective for a different learner. This can be a challenge for strategic scrutiny since boards typically receive information at a grouped level. The good news is that governors and trustees will already be receiving information that can help them to provide an appropriate level of support and challenge in relation to provision and outcomes for learners with DME. In some cases, existing reporting templates can be adapted to ensure they include a focus on DME.

The first question a board of governors or trustees might ask themselves is whether all members of the board can name the four broad areas of need from the SEND Code of Practice 2015 and whether they can articulate what is meant by High Learning Potential. It may also be appropriate for board members to understand the four DME profiles introduced in the DME matrix in Chapter 1 (Figure 1.3). Such knowledge will help boards to stop thinking of learners with DME as a homogeneous group and will facilitate a more nuanced and informed approach to strategic decision-making. This is not the full extent of DME knowledge that board members should have, but it is a reasonable minimum expectation.

The 'Governance Handbook' (DfE, 2019b) identifies the six key features of effective school governance as:

1. **Strategic leadership** that sets and champions vision, ethos and strategy.
2. **Accountability** that drives up educational standards and financial performance.
3. **People** with the right skills, experience, qualities and capacity.
4. **Structures** that reinforce clearly defined roles and responsibilities.
5. **Compliance** with statutory and contractual requirements.
6. **Evaluation** to monitor and improve the quality and impact of governance.

In the context of DME, governors and trustees should be looking for evidence of the following:

1. **Strategic leadership** that sets and champions vision, ethos and strategy.
    - The identification of DME should be built into the overall approach to monitoring the progress and development of all learners.
    - Statutory policies should work for learners with DME. This includes policies on: Special Educational Needs, Admissions Arrangements, Accessibility Plans, Supporting Pupils with Medical Conditions, Equality Information and Objectives, School SEN Information Report.
2. **Accountability** that drives up educational standards and financial performance.
    - Board members should question leaders on how the in-school assessment system in use effectively supports the attainment and progress of all pupils, including those with DME.
    - At least one board member (perhaps the SEND governor and/or gifted and talented governor) should have a more in-depth knowledge of the requirements related to the education of learners with DME. It may be appropriate to appoint a DME lead governor.
    - The impact of financial resources spent on supporting learners with DME should be well understood by the board.
3. **People** with the right skills, experience, qualities and capacity.
    - The annual skills audit should explicitly identify board development needs in relation to DME.
    - The board should have access to expert advice in relation to DME.
4. **Structures** that reinforce clearly defined roles and responsibilities.
    - DME should be clearly positioned as a core responsibility of an appropriate subcommittee so that there is effective scrutiny.
    - Reporting templates should include DME as standard practice where appropriate.
5. **Compliance** with statutory and contractual requirements.
    - SEND Code of Practice 2015.
    - Equality Act 2010 (including reasonable adjustments).
    - Children and Families Act 2014.
6. **Evaluation** to monitor and improve the quality and impact of governance.
    - Board self-evaluation should include a DME element.
    - External perspectives on the strategic approach to DME should be sought, valued and acted upon.

Boards that are reviewing their approach to effective DME governance can consider this simple question: at board level, does DME have the same status as Pupil Premium? The statutory requirements in relation to Pupil Premium are such that board members generally have a good understanding of how many pupils are eligible for Pupil Premium, how the ring-fenced funding has been spent and whether or not the funded provision has been effective. The scrutiny and monitoring for DME could and should be on par with that of Pupil Premium.

In practical terms, boards receive an annual report in relation to Pupil Premium and this should provide them with the information that they need to offer appropriate support and challenge. This reporting template could easily be adapted to include learners with SEND, High Learning Potential and DME. The overlap between learners with DME and those eligible for Pupil Premium is of particular interest since it could be argued that they are double disadvantaged and triple funded. Double disadvantaged in the sense that they have DME and are eligible for Pupil Premium. Triple funded in the sense that they may attract the standard age-weighted pupil funding, Pupil Premium funding and an element of the notional SEN budget. It is not unreasonable for governors and trustees to seek reassurance that this triple funding is being used in a complementary way and having the required impact.

All board members must be able to question school leaders on the attainment and progress of learners with DME. As a starting point, if board members do not feel confident in answering the following questions, this should prompt some key discussions at the next board meeting.

- How successful is our school in meeting the needs of pupils with DME so that they achieve good outcomes? How do we know?
- If outcomes are not good, is this a resourcing (e.g. staff numbers, competence, professional development requirements or classroom resources and equipment) issue?
- What are the barriers to further improvement and even better outcomes for children with DME?
- What actions could the board take to ensure that priorities address any barriers and challenges concerning DME?

The National Governance Association identifies eight elements of effective governance (NGA, 2019) and the list below considers each of them in the context of DME.

1. **The right people round the table**: recruitment of trustees/governors who support a pro-DME ethos and will be able to understand DME issues.
2. **Understanding the role and responsibilities**: induction covers DME and the appointment of a SEND or other trustee/governor explicitly includes DME.
3. **Good chairing**: ensures the board carries out SEND duties and recognises DME and High Learning Potential.
4. **Professional clerking**: arranges induction which covers SEND, High Learning Potential and DME.
5. **Good relationships based on trust**: a code of conduct observed – there are no personal agendas that may jeopardise the pursuit of excellence for learners with DME.
6. **Knowing the school**: this includes knowing the data related to SEND, High Learning Potential and DME; having a good knowledge of staff, families, children and the wider community; having access to quality data and other information (e.g. surveys, complaints).
7. **Committed to asking challenging questions**: including progress and attainment for learners with DME.
8. **Confident to have courageous conversations in the interests of the children and young people**: following up when required to ensure impact.

Other data that is routinely provided to boards and could provide an insight to the quality of DME provision includes:

- Progress and attainment data. What is the value added for learners with the highest levels of baseline attainment? Is the data for learners with DME available in an explicit format?
- Exclusions data. Have any learners with DME been excluded? Were their DME needs being appropriately met?
- Unauthorised absence rates. High levels of unauthorised absence may suggest an issue of family confidence. What follow-up has there been in relation to unauthorised absence?
- Leader, workforce and family voice. Is there confidence in DME provision at all levels of the school community?

Summary

Leadership and governance that has an explicit focus on DME can be an influential factor in ensuring that the needs of all learners are met so that they have the best chance of reaching their full potential. Whilst policies, processes and procedures all have an important role to play, it is the culture and ethos of inclusion and the personal values of leaders that will have the most significant impact for learners with DME. If DME is not deemed important enough for leaders to focus on, then how can we expect the wider workforce to acknowledge its importance. For truly effective DME provision, every leader must be a leader of DME.

Box 3.2 Ten myths of supporting pupils with DME

Myth No. 5: Abilities and Special Educational Needs cannot be addressed at the same time.

To enable DME pupils to succeed, both their HLP and their SEND must be addressed at the same time. However, unlike most deficit-based models where the Special Educational Needs or Disabilities are supported first, this should be through a strengths-based model where the Special Educational Needs are supported through the abilities or skills. For example, a pupil who is passionate about football but who has issues with writing might be encouraged to write about what he or she is good at, whilst being helped to support their handwriting.

Myth No. 6: Pupils with DME cannot go onto our school's HLP programme, they would slow down the other pupils.

Making accommodations in how a subject is taught to make it easier for a child or young person with DME to learn (e.g. using technology) does not affect what is learnt so it will have no impact on the school's programme for its HLP pupils. If anything, going into a higher-level class, if the pupil is supported in the right way, can increase their motivation to learn and can help with progress and achievement.

Notes

1 www.gov.uk/guidance/complete-the-school-census/census-dates.
2 www.gov.uk/government/collections/statistics-special-educational-needs-sen#national-statistics-on-special-educational-needs-in-england.
3 https://iqmaward.com.
4 www.nace.co.uk/page/challenge-award.
5 www.potentialplusuk.org/index.php/schools/hlp-best-practice-award.

4   Effective relationships with learners and their families

His parents say that our pupil (aged 6) has high ability and we recognise that he is very good at maths. However, he is completely unwilling to write things down. I mean one sentence on a page. If there is trouble in the class, he is usually the cause and I find myself telling him off. What can I do?

(Teacher)

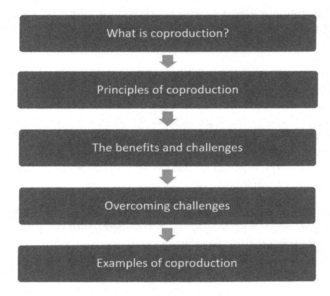

Figure 4.1

One of the central aims of the Children and Families Act 2014 was to ensure that the services delivered consistently placed children, young people and their parents/carers at the centre of the decision-making process. For families with children or young people with DME this includes ensuring that there is a clear approach which involves the participation of children and young people and their parents/carers in making decisions about how best to support their SEND at both an individual and strategic level.

Involving children and young people and parents/carers as equal and meaningful partners in DME provision goes beyond their involvement or engagement in education towards genuine coproduction. Effective coproduction can bring many benefits to the school and to the families involved. This chapter demonstrates how effective coproduction with learners and families can personalise provision and help the school to develop and implement a more effective strategy for DME.

What is coproduction?

Although the term 'coproduction' has been in use for almost 40 years, there is little consensus about what it means and what effective coproduction looks like.

The New Economics Foundation (nef) and Nesta in the publication 'The Challenge of Coproduction' defined coproduction as follows:

'Coproduction means delivering public services in an equal and reciprocal relationship between professionals, people using the services, families and neighbours.'

(Boyle and Harris, 2009)

In education, this goes beyond the active involvement of children and young people, their parents or carers and respects and builds into the process their knowledge, skills and experience so that it feeds into and shapes the process itself.

How is this relevant for children/young people with DME and their parents/carers?

Parents and carers often discover early on that their child is 'different'. This can be seen in different ways:

- In the strengths their child shows, for example early reading, advanced vocabulary, mathematical abilities, advanced verbal abilities or through their vivid imagination.
- In the difficulties their child seems to have such as their inability to interact on the same social or emotional level as their peer group or their late talking skills.
- In any special need they appear to exhibit such as their intensity or obsession with specific subjects (some common ones are dinosaurs, the planets, animals, mathematics, literature) or their potential inability to hear.

What the parent/carer or school does next generally depends upon a range of factors including whether:

- the child has other siblings for the parent/carer to reference their development;
- they see their child and how they interact with other children of the same age at playgroup, nursery or elsewhere;
- they, the early years setting, another professional (e.g. a health visitor) or a friend/colleague has experience of HLP or SEND or both.

All of this usually leads to the parent/carer going down either the 'SEND route' or the 'HLP route' to try to understand what is happening with their child. However, for many parents or carers, they can feel as if they have soon reached a dead end as their child does not fit into either one group or the other. Many are told when their child is at a particularly young age that the issue is a developmental one and that they will 'grow out of it'. However, increasingly concerned by their child's development, they often turn to research or professional help for answers. This can often lead nowhere as there are comparatively few specialists in the UK who specialise in identifying or recommending support for children or young people with DME.

When the child starts school, the work they are expected to do becomes more and more difficult. Their coping mechanisms at this stage can become increasingly more extreme, such as kicking, biting, screaming or having emotional meltdowns. This can lead to increasing isolation and frustration or emotional or mental health problems. In responding, the school may start to go down the SEND route to seek an explanation for what is going on, missing the fact that the child has DME.

By the time the parent/carer is built back into the picture, they can have pent-up frustration or anger that no one can see all sides of their child, including their strengths and the things they find to be a challenge, and they may not know what is going on both with their child and the support provided to them or required. Conversely, at this stage, parents and carers and children and young people may have built up knowledge, skills and experience. These will be useful to the school if they are going to be effective coproducers. The key for professionals is to tap into these.

Every learner is unique and so there is no single approach to DME that will work in every case, but effective relationships with learners and their families can help to personalise provision and an open-door policy on behalf of the school is particularly essential.

Whilst involving the child or young person and their parent/carer effectively in coproduction should apply to every child, and certainly to every child with SEND, there are several issues which must be considered in coproduction with the family of a child with DME:

- The difference in characteristics presented by different children with DME makes 'one size fits all' solutions difficult.
- DME is often difficult to identify.
- There is often a discrepancy between a child or young person's behaviour at school and at home.

- Parents/carers may have a high level of knowledge about DME.
- The child/young person with DME often has strong views about their own needs/potential and an insight into what to do about them. They may be highly able in communicating these views and this can make them invaluable as part of the coproduction process. In many cases, not involving them could be a recipe for disaster.

Box 4.1 An introduction to Joanna

Joanna is 10 years old. She is the youngest of four children and all of her siblings are boys. For a variety of reasons, Joanna ended up in the care system from a young age, initially with a series of foster carers, until she was ultimately adopted. However, the adoption broke down and Joanna went back into long-term foster care.

During this time, there were numerous upheavals at both home and school and by the time she was 8 years old, Joanna had already had six changes of school and was now starting at her seventh. All these schools were one-form entry mainstream primary schools, except for her current school, which is two-form entry. Joanna and her foster parents feel she is making accelerated progress in her current school in a way that they think would have been very difficult to achieve in any of the six previous schools. The foster parents are of the opinion that the provision at Joanna's current school is more effective because the teachers treat Joanna as an individual, rather than just another pupil, and they are committed to meeting her specific individual needs.

Joanna's experiences are such that she has had multiple layers of trauma to deal with, particularly in relation to separation and loss, but she has also demonstrated incredible levels of resilience. Prior to the identification of DME, Joanna had been written off by the teachers in her previous schools as a failure, but over time her High Learning Potential has become more obvious as a result of teachers at her current school and her current foster family recognising and nurturing her High Learning Potential.

Read Joanna's full story in Chapter 5.

How is coproduction different from other types of engagement?

For the purposes of exploring coproduction, the parent and carer, and the child and young person, have been abbreviated into the term 'user' of the services provided by the school, in this instance for DME pupils.

Over the years, there have been several terms used to define user participation in aspects of the school environment. The main ones are represented as a continuum in the diagram below.

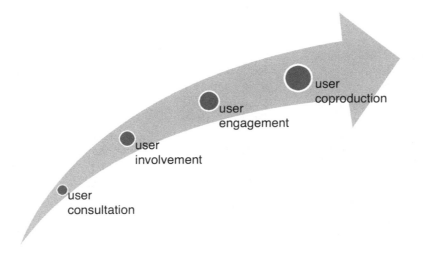

Figure 4.2

In the past, schools might have talked at various times about child or parental consultation, involvement and even engagement. Coproduction is the next logical step. Coproduction recognises that parents/carers and pupils are equal meaningful partners in the development and delivery of education, both individually and strategically. Their involvement is even more proactive, with their knowledge, skills and experience used to shape and make the services delivered more effective.

Effective coproduction can take place on several different levels:

- at an individual level, for example within an assessment or review meeting;
- at a whole school level, for example with the development of a policy and approach on DME;
- at a strategic level, for example in the development of a local authority-wide DME strategy within the Local Offer.

This means that at a school or even local authority level, the views, wishes and feelings of children and young people and their parents/carers must be heard and form part of the process. It is also important to use the knowledge, skills and experience of children and young people and their families to enhance the quality of provision. Finally, becoming an equal meaningful partner should be made as easy as possible. This is particularly true where there may be barriers to this input so that the child or young person, their parents/carer, the school and the local authority can contribute to the best possible educational outcomes and prepare the individual for adulthood.

However, coproduction does not only involve the relationship between teacher, parents/carer and child or young person. In reality it involves a complex matrix of different professionals each with different aims and objectives, frameworks, needs, budgets and restrictions. This can be most clearly seen in the meetings to discuss a child's EHC plan. Notwithstanding, the principles of coproduction, whilst complicated by this matrix of separate issues, should ultimately still remain that parents/carers are equal reciprocal partners in the process.

The example below uses the assessment process of the child or young person to illustrate the point. In this example, the user is the parent or carer or, as appropriate, the child or young person. The professional could mean any professional involved in the process of assessment or provision.

Table 4.1

	Pupil and Parent/ Carer Consultation	Pupil and Parent/ Carer involvement	Pupil and Parent/ Carer Engagement	Pupil and Parent/ Carer Coproduction
Involvement	Passive	Often proactive	Proactive	Proactive
Input of views	Sought	Sought	Provided	Users can express views, wishes and feelings
Framework for views	Provided by professional	Provided by professional	In discussion with user	Devised by professional and user
Interpretation of input	Professional	Professional	Professional with some input from user	User and professional working together
Writing of report	Professional	Professional with feedback from user	Professional with feedback from user	User and professional
Decision-making	Professional	Professional with input from user	Professional with input from user	User and professional
Ownership of report	Professional	Professional with involvement of user	Professional with support from user	User and professional joint ownership
Identification of barriers	Professional if sought	Professional once user input provided	Professional following engagement with users	User or professional
Removal of barriers	Professional	Professional	Professional with engagement from key users	User or professional depending on barrier

	Pupil and Parent/ Carer Consultation	Pupil and Parent/ Carer involvement	Pupil and Parent/ Carer Engagement	Pupil and Parent/ Carer Coproduction
Training	Professional	Professional	Professional sometimes on the recommendation of users	User or professional depending on need
Monitoring/ evaluation	Generated by professional with specified input from user	Generated from professional but directed involvement from user	Input from professional and user usually specified but may be from user	User or professional or both monitor and evaluate and recommend
Finance/budget	Professional	Professional	Professional sometimes on the recommendation of users	User or professional depending on need and circumstances

This table shows some of the distinctions between different types of user engagement. The main differences can be seen in how passive or proactive the users are and how much of a lead the professional takes in directing the areas under investigation or resulting documents drawn up within the assessment.

In consultation, for example, the whole framework is devised and directed by the professional and they decide what the users will be asked, how and when. Contrast that with coproduction, where the user is actively involved in the process from devising the framework, to identifying what the gaps or barriers are and helping to put together the strategy and work to address them.

In the first column (consultation), teachers or other professionals may decide that a certain psychologist should do all the assessments of the potential children or young people with DME at the school. In the fourth column (coproduction), the parents/carers may identify that a psychologist is needed and may identify who that should be. They may then work with the school to make sure a budget is allocated for this. Alternatively, they may put in place a programme of training the existing psychologist in how to identify and provide appropriate recommendations to support children or young people with DME in the school.

The principles of effective person-centred coproduction for DME

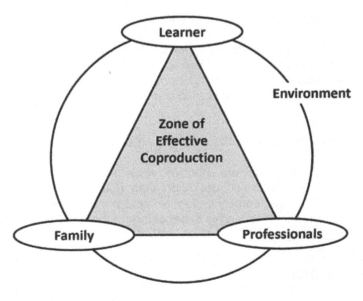

Figure 4.3 Zone of effective coproduction.

Effective person-centred, coproduction in DME education should involve the following general principles:

1. Respect for everyone's values, preferences, views, wishes and feelings and the encouragement of an open, honest and constructive dialogue.
2. Children, young people and parents/carers should be an equal, meaningful part of the decision-making process.
3. Everyone should be involved in the development of a holistic, strengths-based approach to DME education.
4. Respect for and accommodation of any learning, emotional and physical needs and appropriate support provided accordingly. This should include emotional support to alleviate any fear and anxiety about the process or the future.

In addition, at an individual level:

5. Support should be tailored to meet the needs of the individual and to enable a smooth transition from one learning situation, class or school to another.
6. Both SEND and HLP professionals or equivalent should be involved as partners in the development of DME strategy to maximise the child or young person's potential and to help ensure emotional and academic well-being.
7. Appropriate and timely information should be provided about the education of a child with DME and how their needs will be met. Any information provided should be appropriately explained and, as far as possible, free from jargon and delivered in a way in which the parent/carer can access, with sufficient opportunity to ask questions about the content of the information and when this will be delivered.
8. Any restrictions preventing successful partnership working should be addressed. This includes any barriers to participation.

All these approaches could be written up in a charter of commitment by the school for circulation to teachers, parents/carers and pupils which clearly states their responsibilities to each other and to which each could hold the others to account if they do not meet the standards set.

The benefits of coproduction

One of the central ideas behind coproduction in schools is that children and young people and their parents/carers are resources whose skills could be proactively used rather than taking up scarce resources within the school itself. At its most effective, coproduction means equal partnership in a school where all resources on an issue are pooled together to provide the best solutions to a problem or issue.

Moving to coproduction is not always easy for either the professionals or the families. Many parents and carers and sometimes even children and young people may not be currently engaged in the school and teachers can face numerous barriers to involving them. However, if it is done in the right way and effort is put in to removing the barriers to coproduction, the benefits can include:

- the delivery of better outcomes for the child, young person and the school;
- greater ownership of issues;
- the prevention of problems and more effective problem-solving;
- an increase in the capacity of the school by bringing in additional resources;
- the expansion of a self-help mentality by families and professionals;
- the encouragement of positive changes in behaviour by both families and professionals.

The challenges of effective parental engagement (coproduction) at school and home and the DME pupil

In many respects, the challenges of working effectively with parents and carers as a professional in school will be the same regardless of whether a child or young person has DME or not and this is an area where good practice for one group can be good practice for the school as a whole.

One of the biggest challenges to coproduction is the mindset of both families and professionals, particularly in an environment where the professional has always done things 'for' the family and where the professional is always seen as the most knowledgeable, skilled or experienced person about a subject or issue.

This can be exacerbated by parents and carers who, for a variety of reasons, face barriers to equal partnership arising from their background or the way they are able to respond to involvement because of their own availability or values base.

For example, some parents/carers may have had negative experiences of their own schooling and this prevents them from wanting to go into school for their own children. Whilst some parents and carers have had positive experiences of their own schooling and expect similar reactions from teachers when they enquire about issues with their own child, the past negative experience of others may be such that they are unwilling to go into school until they are extremely anxious or angry about an issue or problem which has arisen. Without care on the part of the school, their experiences can become a self-fulfilling prophecy which helps no one, particularly their child.

Some parents and carers may not understand how schools work, particularly in terms of speed of decisions and action, all of the acronyms and the right people to see. Parents and carers sometimes remark that they struggle to understand who to go and see when an issue has arisen, how to make an approach and the right time to do it. They may leave an issue until it becomes almost impossible to solve and the relationship has broken down, such as when their child drops out of school or is at risk of exclusion.

Whilst many parents and carers are able to go into school to seek the resolution of an issue, there can be a lack of confidence amongst others. One of the reasons for this could include the parents/carers own lack of skills or even their own Special Educational Needs including difficulties in reading or writing. It is not unheard of, for example, for a parent to come in about their child's suspected autism spectrum condition, for them to be later identified as being on the spectrum themselves.

Other parents/carers may be daunted by documents that use complicated language or jargon they hear from professionals when they go to a meeting. Where there are barriers in terms of their own skills (reading or writing for example) or language difficulties (if English is not their first language) it can make it difficult to pass on their knowledge and skills. How many parents/carers may be too embarrassed to say they do not have a computer or do not know how to use one and so just nod when they are told something will be emailed to them?

As with many teachers, parents and carers can often become anxious when they meet to solve a difficult issue in school. However, one size really does not fit all, particularly in the areas of SEND, HLP and DME. By the time many parents/carers come into school they have already done extensive research themselves and may know more on the issue than the teacher or other professional. Others are doctors, psychologists and teachers in their professional life. It is essential to listen to what they say and to be open-minded so as to benefit from their research and the information provided within the context of your own school.

Therefore, whilst most parents/carers will be able to play a part in coproduction, it is still essential that the language used by everyone is clear and easily understood, and that documents are written well without the overuse of acronyms or jargon and without being patronising.

In addition, there may be other practical barriers to effective coproduction which need to be considered in relation to the school's overall coproduction strategy. For example, parents and carers may work long hours, shifts or have other working patterns which make it difficult to engage with teachers during the school's time frame. Many schools are developing innovative approaches towards making it easier for parents/carers to engage with them, including the use of technology.

There could be a variety of other reasons that make parents and carers harder to reach, including distance from the school or where one of the parents is in prison or works overseas. These, and any other barriers, must be taken into account in encouraging effective parental coproduction.

One of the first things which might need to happen in the development of a coproduction strategy for children and young people with DME is an honest discussion about any barriers and how they can be overcome.

This should include an initial evaluation by both teachers and parents/carers about issues such as how, where and when coproduction could occur, the most appropriate language to use, the depth into which they go into an issue and the kind of questions they can ask. Getting this coproduction framework right is essential.

In terms of language and terminology, for example, pitching at too high a level may lead to confusion. However, pitching at too low a level can come across as patronising. Devising a standard form for the school to use which asks an initial set of questions about an issue will enable professionals, parents and carers and also children and young people to understand the level and depth with which to talk about these issues.

Taking a critical look at the barriers affecting coproduction both amongst children and young people and parents and carers is being done in schools up and down the country and has led over the years to a range of varied responses including setting up GCSE classes in the school for parents and carers to help meet basic skill needs and improve their confidence, running consultation events via Skype and running training sessions for parents and carers at a local football club.

In addition to any barriers which may affect every child and young person, there are some barriers which will need to be considered individually for a child with DME, although they may apply to other groups of children such as those with HLP and SEND. These may include additional difficulties in identification or disagreements about characteristics contributing to DME leading to greater stress, anxiety or frustration on the part of the parent/carer, child/young person, teacher or other professional.

In the area of SEND and HLP there can often be difficulties in accurate identification. However, in a DME pupil, these issues can be even more difficult to identify without the right training or experience around these children. This is because of how the Special Educational Needs and high abilities interact with each other; sometimes cancelling each other out and sometimes showing one at the expense of the other. Often, by the time parents and carers come into school they have been looking for a solution, perhaps for many years, which addresses their child's needs or helps to predict how they will act in a particular situation and they are looking for the teacher or other professional attached to the school to provide the answers.

In addition, the child may be 'erratically different'. Many children with DME have asynchronous development, whereby they are more advanced in some things (e.g. their intellectual ability) and further behind in others (e.g. their social and emotional maturity). Many parents/carers, teachers and other professionals remark that they do not feel they know the child at all. Sometimes their 7-year-old will be talking about Plato or Pythagoras' Theorem and they could mistake them for a 15-year-old; the next minute they are having a tantrum or biting their sister or classmates and could be mistaken for a 3-year-old.

Within a child with DME, this behaviour is usually not as a result of the child being spoilt or undisciplined (although the responses to it may reinforce this behaviour over time), but can be a natural part of growing up for an asynchronous child and should reduce or be brought under control as the child gets older particularly if the teacher and parent/carer work together on a consistent approach which helps the child or young person to achieve this.

The child may be different at school or at home and both professionals and parents/carers need to listen, understand and piece together what is happening to the whole child. For example, sometimes at school, a child with DME will bottle up the frustration and anger they feel because their learning difficulties are acting as a barrier to their abilities and what they feel they should be capable of achieving. At school, the teacher may be presented with an average child or young person, often someone who is quiet and gets on with their work.

However, at home, the child's frustration bubbles up 'like a pressure cooker exploding' and they are extremely poorly behaved or have extreme emotional outbursts. This child may be inappropriately referred to as a 'teacher pleaser' who wants to fit in with expectations but who knows they can let these frustrations out at home. Only in extreme circumstances will the teacher see the behaviour the parents or carers see all the time at home.

The opposite is also true with the child who has emotional or behavioural issues at school, but when they are at home and they are able to follow subjects about which they are passionate rather than those dictated by the school, they quieten down and are content.

Both types of scenario are common for a child with DME. However, when teachers and parents/carers meet for the first time they often do not recognise the 'other child' being described. This is where it is essential to keep an open mind and ensure that there is active listening on both sides to put together a picture of the whole child. This will enable the child with DME to move forward in their education at school.

Finally, in looking for solutions to DME issues, it must be remembered that children with DME can often have strong views about the issues they experience; views which may even conflict with those of their parents/carers. Many of these children and young people, sometimes from a very young age, have been 'in charge', determining what they will or will not do. By the time parents and carers become involved with the school, matters can have got out of hand. This can prove to be a significant barrier to coproduction or even in matters related to the child or young person's education or attendance at school, and needs to be handled in a sensitive way.

Overcoming challenges

The Education Endowment Foundation guidance report 'Working with Parents to Support Children's Learning' (Poortvliet et al., 2018) recommends four key things which schools should do:

1. Critically review how they work with parents and carers.
2. Provide practical strategies to support learning.
3. Tailor school communications to encourage positive dialogue about learning.
4. Offer more sustained and intensive support where needed.

For the parents/carers of children and young people with DME, the following additional suggestions are recommended:

5. Keep an open mind about the issues which parents/carers of children or young people with DME, or potential DME, may raise.
6. Actively listen to parent/carers of children with DME to enable a holistic picture to be built up about what is happening to the child at school and at home.
7. Create an environment where there can be a mutually open and honest discussion about the needs of the child or young person and work positively with the whole family to problem-solve the issues which have been raised.
8. Tap into the knowledge, skills and experience of parents/carers of children with DME and work with them to develop clear strategies to support their child.

Examples of coproduction with DME families

Some schools have already developed new and imaginative ways to take forwards elements of coproduction with their parents/carers or children or young people with DME. In addition to coproduction, which benefits the individual child or young person with DME, some ideas which schools could further develop include:

- **Specialist DME volunteers** – parents/carers who can provide knowledge and experience to advise other parents on DME issues within the school. These parents/carers could be trained by the school to an approved standard (including on the school's policies towards DME) and this would provide help in increasing school support capacity. The same approach could be taken towards young people.
- **Trained mediators** – mediators could be trained at a variety of different levels to provide help to schools in resolving disagreements about DME or the support received (or not received).
- **Trainers** – parents/carers (or young people) could be trained and provided with the skills to raise awareness within the school about DME or aspects of DME, such as identification or supporting a child with DME at school or home.
- **DME strategy team** – a team made up of parents/carers, learners and professionals could be responsible for researching, setting, monitoring and evaluating the school's strategy for DME on behalf of the board of governors or trustees. This could also be done on a wider level for a group of academies or for a local authority.

Summary

Coproduction is an integral component of the Children and Families Act (2014). The proactive involvement of parents and carers and, as appropriate, children and young people can lead to a range of benefits for all parties. However, there are numerous challenges to be overcome to ensure that an equal and reciprocal relationship is developed which builds on the unique skills, knowledge, views and perspectives of all parties. To facilitate this, these challenges must be addressed openly and with consideration. This includes any specific issues faced by schools and by families with a child or young person who has DME. If this can be done through open and honest dialogue it will lead to a positive impact on those pupils who have DME.

Some real stories of DME pupils, their families and how schools have supported them can be found in the next chapter.

Box 4.2 Ten myths of supporting pupils with DME

Myth No. 7: Addressing the pupil's weaknesses must be the top priority for our pupils with DME.

Some approaches to SEND support prioritise addressing a pupil's areas of weakness rather than building on their strengths. However, this approach can impact on the self-confidence and self-esteem of a pupil with DME, making them less likely to want to learn or to tackle the difficult issues. They need teachers and other professionals who believe in what they can do and can help them to improve their strengths to support the areas in which they struggle. Examples of how to do this are provided throughout this book and particularly in the stories in Chapter 5.

Myth No. 8: Pupils with DME should be more mature than other pupils their own age.

One of the biggest myths is that pupils with DME are mature in every aspect of their lives. However, children and young people with DME often have asynchronous development where they are ahead in some things (usually their intellectual maturity) and behind in others (usually their social and emotional maturity). Such asynchronous development can make it hard for them to build relationships with other children of their own age.

---

5 DME provision
Real stories

We believe that she is working well at school but feel that she has underlying issues at school and home including struggling with light and noise when she is trying to work. She blurts out the answers to questions and interrupts a lot and we have found it difficult for her to do group work as she asks too many questions. We don't know what to do.

(Teacher)

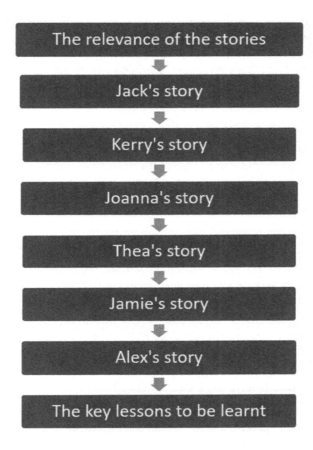

Figure 5.1

The relevance of the stories

Children and young people with DME are not easy to identify, and their needs can be even harder to determine, both within and outside the classroom. Every pupil is an individual and their abilities and needs even more so. It is the job of the teacher, working alongside those other professionals within the school (as well as parents or carers and the child or young person themselves), to enable every pupil to achieve to the best of their capabilities in a way which maximises their strengths and supports the issues which challenge them.

To best illustrate what is happening within schools up and down the country, the following six stories have been shared. Each of these stories is based on real children and young people at different stages within the education process and the children and their families have given permission for their stories to be shared. We have changed the children's names to protect their real identities and respect their privacy. Each story provides a snapshot of the journey of the pupil and what has helped (or hindered) them along the way. Each story has been written in a slightly different way to capture the different people who helped write them. Some, for example, principally involved teachers in the drafting, some involved parents or carers and in others the voice of the child or young person can be clearly heard. Notwithstanding, they are evaluated under similar headings to enable a comparison to be made between each of them.

None of these pupils' journeys is over and each child may face further triumphs or set-backs as they move through the education system and beyond. Nonetheless they each provide an evaluation of the kinds of things that work and do not work for children and young people with DME within the school system.

At the end of this chapter, a summary is provided for schools about the kinds of things that they should be considering to support their DME cohort. It is not an exhaustive list but is based on the practical ideas emerging from these real stories.

Many teachers may be doing these things already and may consider them merely good practice for all their pupils, including those with DME, in the school. If that is the case, that is positive news and shows that support for these pupils can be easily incorporated into current practice within existing resourcing levels.

On the other hand, the stories may provide a selection of practical ideas which can be built into the current curriculum for every child or offered to specific groups such as those in danger of exclusion from school.

Either way, it is hoped that, in most cases, these practical recommendations can be implemented within current resourcing levels and structures or with targeted funding to meet an individual's specific needs.

Jack's story

> ### Box 5.1
>
> **What are his specific strengths?** General high ability
>
> **What are his specific needs?** Autism and Sensory Processing Disorder along with a discrepancy between verbal and nonverbal reasoning.
>
> **Schooling:** Nursery and state primary school.

Introduction to the child and the context

Right from when he first started nursery, Jack's behaviour has been difficult for the school to deal with. He would stand still and scream, making it very hard to divert his attention away from any task he wanted to undertake.

Jack had low social awareness and interaction with peers. Instead, he talked to adults as equals and on occasion tried to demand their attention regardless of the time or place. It was also difficult to gauge Jack's true ability as he frequently refused to complete tasks without one-to-one support. Whilst still at nursery, Jack was put on the SEND register for behaviour support and strategies.

After a difficult time at nursery, Jack continued to display challenging behaviour at the start of primary school. However, Jack was imaginative, loved playing board-games and learning facts, and he had a boundless passion for mathematics. Jack's parents recognised that they needed to have a better understanding of his areas of strength, as they didn't want all the focus to be only on his difficulties at the expense of other things.

Identification of DME

The need to identify Jack's strengths, led his parents to seek out Potential Plus UK, a charity with expertise in supporting children and young people with High Learning Potential, including children and young people with DME. With support from Potential Plus UK's advisory service and following an in-depth assessment, it was soon established that Jack has DME and that his High Learning Potential was combined with some form of learning disability.

In Jack's case it combined cognitive functioning on the 99th percentile with diagnoses of Autistic Spectrum Condition and Sensory Processing Disorder. In addition, there was a significant difference between his ability in verbal and nonverbal reasoning, which impacted upon his motivation and consistency of attainment.

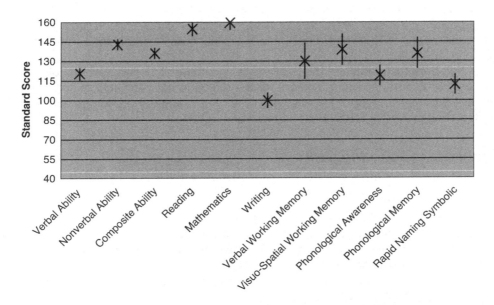

Figure 5.2

Description of DME provision

Jack is now 10 years old and in Year 5 of a state primary school. Over the years, Jack's parents and school have formed a close, supportive relationship. His parents were relieved when his school took note of the information provided about Jack's cognitive abilities and the recommendations made by Potential Plus UK. They have continued to have confidence in his school:

> 'even when they haven't known what to do, they have listened, understood and worked with us to find a way forward'.

Jack's school has implemented a variety of strategies and adaptations to offer him suitable accommodation and challenge, ranging from older children acting as buddies in the playground and study partners; to ear defenders and fidget toys; chess club and maths acceleration. They have involved outside agencies like the Special Educational Needs Advisory Service (SENAS), speech and language therapists (SALTs) and an occupational therapist. They have also helped Jack's parents to apply for and receive an Education, Health and Care (EHC) plan (a statutory SEND support plan in England) with funding for a part-time teaching assistant from Year 2 (approximately age 7).

At home, his parents have actively sought out opportunities for Jack to mix with similar ability peers and develop his strengths, as well as the areas with which he struggles.

Despite all the support in school, Jack still struggles when there is a lack of challenge in his work, particularly in maths. Having now 'outgrown' primary level maths, this lack of challenge has had a negative impact on his mental health. His school is now looking into options with the local secondary school and a dedicated 'more able' maths tutor.

Adding to Jack's mental health issues is his developing awareness of the differences between himself and his classmates, which has led to a reluctance to mix with his school peers. With continued engagement from Potential Plus UK, Jack's parents and his school are exploring ways they can support him intellectually and emotionally.

Impact of DME provision

Both Jack's teachers and his parents are aware of the need to build on Jack's strengths as well as to address the challenges he faces. They are aware that this is not a one-off intervention but an ongoing dialogue between school and home and, increasingly, with Jack himself. This is seen as important by everyone because of the recognition that, as Jack gets older, his needs and issues will change. This will be particularly the case as he transitions from one school to the next.

Despite the strengths identified, the challenges Jack face still made an EHC plan application possible to provide an ongoing framework for the dialogue between school and home, and his parents have had a strong input in passing on their knowledge and findings about Jack to the school which has proved a positive experience for everyone.

Summary of key learning points

What is the school offer?

As far as possible, provision (such as the school buddy and simple equipment like the ear defenders and computer programmes) was built into current school provision or resources. However, support for additional resources through an EHC plan allowed them to bring in an occupational therapist, SENAS and speech and language therapy.

What are the strengths of this approach?

The main strengths which the school has shown are its open-mindedness and willingness to work with Jack's parents/carers. This has included openness on behalf of the teachers, saying that they do not know about an issue and listening and asking questions until they have understood Jack's DME. This will stand them in good stead for the development of the school's coproduction strategy. The concept of DME is not widely understood and is even more difficult to identify, and just listening to the parent or carer and learning from their research can give them the confidence that they will help support their child in the right way.

What could have been done differently?

Earlier intervention might have saved all three parties – Jack, his teachers and the school and his parents – from a great deal of stress and anxiety about the best way to support Jack. Identification of his strengths and needs could have happened in nursery so that a plan was in place before he started school.

Transition to secondary school is also often difficult for children who have DME, particularly those who also have emotional or mental health issues. Early plans to help Jack with this transition would be useful. Once a place to his secondary school has been awarded, this could also include building on his strengths once more by visiting the school premises for maths tuition. Smaller class sizes and a similar attitude as his primary school might also be part of the choice criteria for where he goes.

Key recommendations for schools

1. Build on the strengths of the child or young person as well as their challenges.
2. Keep an open mind about the information which parents/carers provide and offer an open door which gives them access, without concern, to exploring what they know.
3. Pool knowledge with parents and carers to get the best outcomes for the child or young person.
4. Be aware that the responses of the child or young person towards their DME may change over time and be flexible in meeting these needs.

Reflection from the authors on effective practice and areas for development/ consideration

This case study is an excellent example of how a school and parent/carer could work together to solve issues with a child which are impacting upon behaviour and preventing learning. There are elements of this case which could be used in other, less extreme situations, such as the provision of fidget toys and ear defenders, or buddying schemes which some primary schools are excellent at providing already.

However, the key to the success of this case appears to be the open-door policy of the school and the open-mindedness of the teachers to listen to the parent/carers and to learn from them or others about an issue. In terms of development, perhaps these teachers and the school could train others in how to address DME in such an effective way!

Kerry's story

Box 5.2

What are her specific strengths? High Learning Potential in singing, gymnastics, mathematics and creative writing.

What are her specific needs? Sensory and emotional needs.

- **Anger issues**: Kerry can become irritated quickly by the smallest of issues and, within a short space of time, can become very angry, resulting in physically pushing/hitting her siblings/parents, grunting and angry body language (e.g. clenched fists, red face). Kerry gets angry quickly, but takes a long time to calm down.
- **Anxiety issues**: Kerry is a perfectionist, so if she makes even a minor mistake in her schoolwork, this can be a trigger for becoming angry or anxious. For example, she will hit herself repeatedly on her forehead.
- **Relationships**: Other children at school know that Kerry can be 'wound up' easily and there is some intentional provoking to see her reaction. This means that Kerry's relationships with her peers can be strained and volatile.
- **Schooling**: Small, maintained primary school.

Introduction to the child and the context

Kerry is 8 years old and is one of three siblings. She attends a one-form entry maintained primary school and reports that she finds every single day a challenge. Kerry has a mature and academically advanced view of the world around her, but she doesn't understand why others can't see things the way that she does. She struggles to cope with her own emotional turbulence and is increasingly frustrated with other people.

Kerry's parents first noticed something wasn't right when she started school and they received contradictory progress reports. The reports showed the highest levels of attainment across all subject areas, but the effort grades were mixed. The school was increasingly contacting Kerry's parents about what they described as 'unacceptable behaviours' both in the classroom and in the playground. By the time Kerry was 7 years old, school life had become very hard for her. She had been excluded from social groups by the parents of her peers and was not invited to birthday parties, when the rest of her class were invited. The school were keeping her inside during break and lunch-times 'for the safety of other children' and they had warned Kerry's parents that she was at risk of school exclusion.

Kerry felt isolated by the position in which she found herself and the challenging behaviours, tantrums and violence started to happen at home as well as at school. When Kerry was angry or upset, she physically lashed out at her siblings and parents and she would grunt and growl. Kerry kicked walls and furniture, slammed doors and stamped up the stairs. Very often, Kerry would hit herself repeatedly in the head when she was angry with herself and she would call herself stupid, blaming herself for not being able to control her emotions and behaviours. Kerry's parents were not sure what to do and they became very concerned when Kerry started saying that she wished she was dead and that she wanted to kill herself. She repeatedly said that she hated herself and thought that everybody around her hated her too because of how she was behaving.

It was during these two years, that some of Kerry's talents really become clear too, although it was not obvious to her parents at the time. Kerry was a creative young girl and she began singing – a lot! Her parents said it was often a challenge to settle Kerry down for bed as she was singing entire musical theatre productions before she went to sleep. She also began to express herself through art, drawing and 3-D modelling using clay. At one point, Kerry's parents thought she might be hyperactive, since she was repeatedly jumping on the sofas and doing cart-wheels immediately after eating. It seemed that she could not stop moving.

Kerry was generally less successful at sports if they required hand–eye co-ordination, such as badminton or golf. She would become frustrated when she couldn't play, and it would trigger strong emotional responses. Kerry was also increasingly unaware of her surroundings, which resulted in clumsy accidents, such as forward rolling into walls, knocking into items of furniture or stubbing her toes on furniture.

At school, Kerry had low levels of tolerance to other people being in her personal space and her response was generally violent. Rather than being sensitive to particular textures, Kerry seemed to crave them. For example, she was often found in school rubbing walls and railings, licking her cutlery and squeezing different fabrics in her hands.

Things began to improve for Kerry when a new class teacher started at the school, who had no prior knowledge of Kerry's behaviours, and gave her a fresh start. Following an incident in which Kerry had an emotional meltdown in the playground, this teacher contacted Kerry's parents to find out how she could help. It was this meeting that led to the school SENCO becoming involved. With the class teacher and the SENCO working collaboratively with Kerry and her parents, a strategy was drawn up to identify and support any Special Educational Needs.

The SENCO arranged for several specialists from the local authority to come into school to observe Kerry and to help to assess her needs. The conclusion was that Kerry was identified as having significant sensory needs with anxiety and some autistic traits. The provision put in place by the school included:

- Lego therapy (to help improve communication and teamworking skills);
- yoga (to help improve mindfulness and well-being);
- nurture groups (to help improve Kerry's self-image);
- termly meetings between the SENCO and the parents.

In the months that followed, there were fewer behavioural incidents, but Kerry became more and more unhappy. She started saying that she didn't want to go to school and whilst she was able to manage her emotions better in school, it was becoming more difficult at home.

Identification of DME

At one of the termly meetings between the SENCO and Kerry's parents, it emerged that Kerry was being denied access to certain activities in school if they deemed her behaviour was not good enough. The activities included things like assembly (where Kerry would sing), playtime (where Kerry would do gymnastics in the playground) and golden time (where Kerry would do art and crafts). The class teacher who instigated these consequences was a newly qualified teacher (NQT) who felt she had to apply the school rules consistently.

The SENCO agreed with the parents that blocking access to such activities was contributing to Kerry's low emotional state and supported the parents in bringing an end to such a punitive approach which failed to recognise her needs. She worked with the class teacher on understanding her duties in relation to reasonable adjustments.

The SENCO explained to the parents that she had recently read about DME and was intending to deliver training on it for all staff. She said that she thought Kerry might have DME and arranged for her to be assessed by an educational psychologist. The local authority would not pay for the assessment, so the school covered the costs directly. The educational psychologist confirmed that Kerry was operating at a level academically above what would be typical for her age.

The educational psychologist and the SENCO both agreed that meeting the Special Educational Needs alone was insufficient and that the High Learning Potential needed to be nurtured too. It also became clear that further professional support was required in relation to strategies for helping Kerry to manage her sensory needs. It was recommended that an occupational therapist should be engaged for this. Sadly, the Headteacher at the school ruled that the school could not afford to fund the occupational therapy sessions and so these costs had to be covered directly by the parents.

Description of DME provision

Fortnightly occupational therapy sessions focused on the development of practical strategies centred on Kerry's High Learning Potential. For example, when Kerry was angry or upset, rather than the focus being on stopping the resulting behaviours, she was instead encouraged to shift her energies into an area where she had developing talents, e.g. art, singing, creative writing and mathematics. The occupational therapist also worked with Kerry to help her frame and assess the scale of the problems she faced, so she could respond appropriately. Using these tools, a small problem, for example, would only require a small response appropriate to the situation. The occupational therapist taught Kerry how to recognise the early warning signs and triggers for her anxiety, so she could regulate her emotions whilst she was still in control. Finally, the occupational therapist helped Kerry to understand the effect of the different forms of sensory stimulation that she craved. Some helped to calm her down, whilst others made her more frantic. Understanding which sensory approaches to use in which situations provided Kerry with a set of useful strategies for use at home and at school.

The SENCO and class teacher jointly delivered a twilight professional development session on DME using Kerry as a case study. The SENCO has explained that some staff are still sceptical about DME and take the view that there should be a zero-tolerance approach to 'undesirable behaviour'. However, the Headteacher and most staff were receptive and willing to embrace a different approach. A key message from the SENCO in the staff training was that behaviour is a form of communication.

In class, Kerry has been permitted to use therapy putty as a calming sensory strategy. The school have also provided Kerry with a range of enrichment opportunities to help nurture her talents, including maths competitions, computer programming, school choir and external singing performances. The class teacher has done some work on inclusion with all the children in the class to try to foster more acceptance of differences and to celebrate diversity. This is still a work in progress.

At home, Kerry's parents have signed her up for a musical theatre club that meets on a Saturday morning. This has given her a new friendship group and, whilst there, she discovered that another girl who attends the club is from the year above at her school. This has helped in school as she is now not over-reliant on the friendship groups within her class. Kerry's parents are encouraging her to use her new-found interest in computers to use the built-in features of PowerPoint to write and record her own musical presentations. Recently, she has produced an interactive presentation on the properties of ravens. At bedtime, audio books have been introduced as a form of sensory stimulation that can be focused on Kerry's areas of interest. Most recently, this has been Harry Potter, with Kerry using the stories as a catalyst for her own creative writing. Interestingly, Kerry's class teacher is an avid Harry Potter fan and so this has created an opportunity to further develop the staff–pupil relationship. Kerry and her mum keep an emotions diary in which they exchange messages about how they are feeling, and this has been a useful outlet for emotional discharge. Kerry has increased the volume of creative tasks she engages with at home. Recently, she created a miniature notebook for her toy elf. Despite being miniature, the attention to detail was incredibly intricate with individual lines on the pages and a glittery binding.

Impact of DME provision

Reflecting on the provision, Kerry said that she felt much happier and the strong emotions of self-loathing had mostly subsided. School is still hard for Kerry and this is primarily an issue with the perspectives of the wider parental community and its acceptance of her 'differences' rather than with the school.

Kerry feels that she is now known for more than just her challenging behaviours and says that she now feels like a person rather than a problem. She appreciates what the school and her parents have put in place for her, but she also shared some frustration with being a recipient of the provision and not having enough opportunity to shape it herself.

Kerry's effort grades have soared, and they are now aligned to the high levels of attainment she has had throughout. Kerry has taken the yoga skills she has learnt at school and applied them at home, often leading family yoga sessions. Over the past 12 months, Kerry has developed a fierce sense of moral purpose and social justice and this was triggered by Sir David Attenborough's campaign about plastic in the oceans, which her class learnt about at school. On the one hand, this has been positive because it has given Kerry an external focus for her to apply her talents. On the other hand, it has been a challenge because she is now holding everybody to account for any of their behaviours that she thinks are destroying the planet. This has been the source of a great many arguments with her siblings.

When asked what her biggest success has been, Kerry says it is the improvement in her badminton skills. She explained that she was not the best at badminton, but before she couldn't hit the shuttlecock and as a result she would immediately get angry and throw her racket across the court. Now that she is better able to regulate her emotions, Kerry can play badminton in the garden with her family and she says this makes her feel happy and included.

Summary of key learning points

What is the school offer?

The school's offer is centred around developing a culture of inclusion for all children, including those with DME, which is customised depending on their specific needs. It has funded a certain amount of work with the child, including the assessment and behavioural programme, and the parents have had to pay for some of the more expensive elements such as ongoing work with the occupational therapist. However, the school has been open and honest about what it can and cannot do. The school has taken the issue of DME through the whole school, including training teachers and other staff.

What are the strengths of this approach?

This approach has worked, despite initial opposition from some members of staff, because of the support and backing of the Headteacher and the existence of a DME Champion within school who has helped to spearhead work in this area, including training others.

The school has increasingly recognised that behaviour is a form of communication and instead of penalising children because of their behaviour, it is trying to focus on the High Learning Potential of the child. The SENCO, class teacher, Headteacher and external professionals have developed a genuine partnership with the parents to ensure a joined-up and co-ordinated approach to the DME provision.

What could have been done differently?

Reflecting on what the school could do differently, it would be to ensure greater consistency of identification and provision across the school. In this case, Kerry's situation improved only when the SENCO, Headteacher and class teacher co-ordinated their efforts. Had there been greater consistency from the outset and a greater awareness of DME, this would have enabled earlier identification to take place.

Key recommendations for schools

1. Ensure that there is a DME policy in place, which will help to create a consistent approach to the identification of DME.
2. Ensure that school leaders and governors support effective DME provision through all elements of the ethos and culture of the school. For example, zero-tolerance approaches to managing behaviour may be incompatible with inclusion and personalised provision.
3. Involve a range of professionals to identify both needs and strengths and to input into the shaping of provision.

Reflection from the authors on effective practice and areas for development/consideration

This case study shows the journey of a very self-aware and creative girl who, at a young age, did not have the emotional maturity to translate her frustration with the suppression of her abilities and 'acted out' this frustration through poor behaviour which got her noticed for the wrong reasons. If it was not for the intervention of the teacher who both recognised Kerry's Special Educational Needs and her HLP and the Headteacher who was prepared to back them, it is likely that this girl would have developed more severe mental health issues in the future.

The role of an advocate of DME is critical to this case. In this instance it was the class teacher who recognised what might have been happening and used their own knowledge to pass on their skills to others within the school. This DME Champion was vital in overcoming initial scepticism, securing resources and support and becoming the 'specialist' to spearhead a school-wide DME initiative which will benefit other children in the future.

It is a shame that, where more specialist provision needed to be made, the school did not have the resources to fund it. This is a common occurrence for many children and young people with Special Educational Needs, in the widest sense, within schools at present. In this instance, the parents were able to pay for the additional provision. What would have happened if they could not find the resources required to support their child? How much worse would the situation have had to get; exclusion or self-exclusion or following through on the threats of self-harm and even suicide?

If DME is to be addressed as a serious issue within schools, appointing a DME Champion within all schools, a Specialist Leader of Education for DME and even a national DME Champion would help to raise awareness of DME and advocate for the needs of this group of children and young people.

Joanna's story

Box 5.3

What are her specific strengths? Sports and music. There may also be significant academic underachievement and unrealised academic potential.

What are her specific needs? Social, emotional and mental health, emotional trauma, post-traumatic stress.

Schooling: Six earlier primary schools prior to her current state primary school.

Introduction to the child and the context

Joanna is 10 years old and has dual heritage. She is the youngest of four children and all of her siblings are boys. Joanna's birth family lived in an area of significant social deprivation and they received parenting from their single mother. For reasons that will not be further explained here, Joanna ended up in the care system from a young age, initially with a series of foster carers, until she was ultimately adopted. However, the adoption broke down and Joanna went back into long-term foster care.

During this time, there were numerous upheavals at both home and school and by the time she was 8 years old, Joanna had already had six changes of school and was now starting at her seventh. All these schools were one-form entry mainstream primary schools, except for her current school, which is two-form entry. Joanna and her foster parents feel she is making accelerated progress in her current school in a way that they think would have been very difficult to achieve in any of the six previous schools. The foster parents are of the opinion that the provision at Joanna's current school is more effective because the teachers treat Joanna as an individual, rather than just another pupil, and they are committed to meeting her specific individual needs.

Joanna's experiences are such that she has had multiple layers of trauma to deal with, particularly in relation to separation and loss, but she has also demonstrated incredible levels of resilience. Prior to the identification of DME, Joanna had been written off by the teachers in her previous schools as a failure, but over time her High Learning Potential has become more obvious as a result of teachers at her current school and her current foster family recognising and nurturing her High Learning Potential.

Identification of DME

The foster family that Joanna is with currently have a strong track record in supporting the identification of Special Educational Needs and in spotting and nurturing the talents of children and young people in their care. In Joanna's case, it was initially thought that there may be elements of attention deficit hyperactivity disorder (ADHD), since she was struggling to sit still in class and to concentrate for any extended periods. However, it later transpired that the child psychologist and the psychotherapist believed that these issues were a result of post-traumatic stress.

In many ways, the Special Educational Needs and the health and care needs were clear from the outset for Joanna because of the knowledge that professionals involved with her already had in relation to her wider circumstances. Professionals from CAMHS (Child and Adolescent Mental Health Services) led on the formal identification of Joanna's needs with input from social workers and her foster family. The needs were primarily centred around social, emotional and mental health needs and a risk of self-harming was also identified. As part of the ongoing identification and assessment of needs, Joanna is being supported through psychotherapy and drama therapy.

In relation to High Learning Potential, it was both the foster family and the school teachers together who led on the identification of different aspects of Joanna's potential.

At home, the foster parents identified Joanna's passion and potential in singing. They noticed that Joanna was singing in a cupboard as she was too embarrassed to sing publicly. They also felt that there were elements from the impact of trauma at play here too. Her foster parents were keen to build Joanna's confidence to sing and they provided several opportunities to do this in safe settings through their family and friends. This included Joanna singing at family events and buying her a karaoke machine for Christmas. They arranged for Joanna to have professional singing lessons and they approached her school to discuss what opportunities they might be able to provide.

As part of the discussions with the school, it became clear that the teachers had identified Joanna's sporting prowess. It was not just the case that she was good at a particular sport, but that she seemed to excel in almost every sport, despite having had limited exposure to sporting opportunities in the past. Joanna's teachers recognised that her resilience and competitive streak were significant strengths for achieving in sport and the teachers responsible for the various sports teams were competing to have Joanna take up their sport. Joanna learnt many new sports through the school including rounders, tennis, basketball, netball, athletics and cross-country running. Winning a variety of sporting competitions had a significant impact on building her self-esteem and Joanna was generally a happier young girl. The school also provided opportunities for Joanna to sing at music festivals.

Whilst there has been no formal testing for Joanna's High Learning Potential, there is a congruence in the views of a range of professionals and additional evidence that supports the existence of High Learning Potential. Joanna's swimming instructor said, after two lessons, that with her swimming ability she could make it to the Olympics. A secondary school in the area requires a musical aptitude test for entry and teachers at that school believe that Joanna will 'pass with flying colours'. Joanna is regularly invited to sing solo performances at public events, including those with deep personal relevance, such as the Looked After Children Awards.

Her teachers comment that whilst Joanna's attainment may be behind in some academic areas, her progress is significantly accelerated to that of her peers and she constantly surprises them with moments of sheer brilliance. Even at the age of 2, Joanna was able to share a whole host of facts about the world as well as being able to articulate the insight that she had into her own domestic challenges and wider circumstances.

Joanna's school has a good track record of identifying Special Educational Needs and the school's ethos is strongly focused on the pursuit of excellence. The school was actively involved with IGGY (the University of Warwick's International Gateway for Gifted Youth) and they have previously supported educational research into effective teaching strategies for gifted children.

Description of DME provision

A key difference between the provision at Joanna's current school and her previous schools is the enhanced focus on her strengths, rather than her behaviours. Joanna is encouraged to increase her engagement around sport and music, and she is praised when she excels in these areas. The relationships that are developed through the pursuit of excellence in sports and music have built a level of trust between Joanna and teachers at the school, which can help in the classroom when there are challenges in relation to Joanna's behaviours.

The school has a traffic light system in place for managing behaviour. All learners begin on green and if there is poor behaviour, the individuals involved are moved to amber and ultimately to red. Learners on red must stand outside the Headteacher's office with nothing to do until the Headteacher speaks to them and decides what the consequence will be. Whilst the affordances and constraints of this approach to behaviour management could fill the entire book, the focus here is on Joanna's experiences.

The reality was that whilst the system was accepted by most learners, it absolutely did not work for Joanna. If she ended up on red, there would be a total meltdown of behaviour that could put her at risk of exclusion.

The school considered this issue carefully. They did not want to change their current approach to behaviour management as they felt it worked for most learners, but they also thought it would be inequitable to give one learner immunity from any consequences.

Following discussions between the foster parents, the Headteacher and Joanna herself, a compromise was reached based on reasonable adjustments. The school agreed that for Joanna there would be a new category in place of red, called 'managing red'. In practical terms, this meant that Joanna would never be in the position that the behaviour management system was triggering meltdowns and the focus shifted from a consequence-driven approach of behaviour management to a therapeutic-driven approach to behaviour management.

When Joanna reaches 'managing red', she has to go to the Headteacher's office in the same way as other learners, but whilst there she has a dedicated place to sit and rather than waiting for her consequence, she is encouraged to work. There had initially been some concern that other children would complain about this, but in practice the other learners have been very supportive. This more individualised approach has made it easier for the teachers and for Joanna.

In a similar way, the school considered its approach to rewarding academic achievement for Joanna. It was decided that offering rewards linked to Joanna's passion in sports and music would incentivise her to improve her effort in the classroom. There are no consequences if academic targets are not met, but the rewards are only available when there have been sufficient effort and/or achievements.

English, in particular, was deemed by her teachers to be Joanna's weakest subject. An English teacher at the nearby secondary school has a therapy dog and Joanna sees this dog (and the English teacher!) regularly as part of the package of provision for meeting her literacy and trauma needs. Joanna and the English teacher have agreed to write a book together. In practice, Joanna writes a page for the book and this is then edited by the English teacher. This will continue until the book is written, although nobody apart from Joanna and her teacher actually knows what the book will be about!

There has been a serious effort to put effective, meaningful and genuine coproduction in place. Routinely this has involved Joanna, her foster parents and her teachers, not just Joanna's current class teacher, but also her form teacher from when she first joined the school who has stayed alongside Joanna throughout to ensure joined-up support. As required, there has also been engagement with the Headteacher, the SENCO, the GATCO and Joanna's social worker. Here are two examples of meetings leading to coproduction in Joanna's case:

Example 1: Transition meeting

As Joanna moved from one year to the next, there was a meeting between the current and incoming class teachers to which Joanna and her foster parents were invited. Challenges and successes of the current year were discussed and any anxieties about the next year were addressed. Email addresses were exchanged to enable slicker communications between home and school.

If there were issues at home, the class teacher would be aware when Joanna arrived and so be better able to put the necessary provision in place from the outset. Similarly, if Joanna had had a challenging day at school, the foster parents were primed and ready to respond as soon as Joanna arrived home. The foster parents have particularly noted that dealing with any issues on the day as they arise and then drawing a line under them has been highly effective in improving Joanna's well-being, since it has significantly reduced the risk of her going to bed worried or anxious. Every child deserves to be able to have a good night's sleep.

Example 2: Residential meeting

The Headteacher convened and chaired a meeting to discuss a residential school trip, which Joanna had said she was worried about. The SENCO, the foster parents and Joanna's social worker were all in attendance. Joanna was aware that the meeting was happening and fed her views into the meeting, but she chose not to attend. The SENCO outlined the provision that the school could put in place to address Joanna's anxieties and any safeguarding concerns were discussed. The proposed provision was further shaped by the foster parents and the social worker and, as a result, Joanna had a positive residential experience.

In terms of wider provision, teachers at the school noted that Joanna's performance in tests was not aligned to what they saw in the classroom. Discussing this further with Joanna, it emerged that in a test situation, she would see others writing much more than she did and panic. This was an issue of self-confidence and of anxiety and linked to the wider trauma needs.

For tests, the school has now put arrangements in place so that Joanna can be in a room without any other learners, should she prefer that. In this situation, her original class teacher stays with her to supervise and this has a further calming and confidence-boosting effect. Joanna's test performances are now reflective of what teachers had seen in the classroom.

Finally, Joanna's current school prides itself on having an excellent repertoire of extra-curricular activities and enrichment opportunities available to all learners. This provision is of vital importance to many learners with DME and it has been one of the key aspects of effective provision for Joanna.

In her previous schools, there were limited extra-curricular activities and Joanna was generally excluded from them, as this was part of the consequences enforced by the school in response to her behaviour. In one school, after-school clubs were only available to learners in Year 5 or Year 6. At her current school, extra-curricular activities are generally free at the point of use and students are encouraged to attend. Joanna typically spends four out of five school days participating in different after-school enrichment activities.

Impact of DME provision

Joanna and her foster parents are of the view that the provision at the school has had a significant positive impact. On a day-to-day basis, Joanna is a happier child, who has a growing friendship group. The school's approach of matching up children with similar profiles of High Learning Potential has worked well in helping Joanna to find others with similar interests. The school also matches up children with abilities in a specific area to other children who want to develop that area, and this has been equally effective in promoting and celebrating academic diversity.

Looking ahead, Joanna now has positive and ambitious aspirations for the future. Her foster parents believe that Joanna could make it to the Olympics or to attend university, both of which Joanna and teachers at her previous schools had thought impossible only a couple of years ago. Whilst Joanna might have had an innate High Learning Potential, there were limited opportunities for it to be realised. Her foster parents believe that she now has both the ability and the opportunity to succeed.

In the classroom, Joanna's academic potential remains invisible to Joanna herself. She sees that she is not as strong as her peers in relation to attainment, but there is little self-recognition of the accelerated progress that she is making. Her teachers are clear that her pace of learning is rapid, and they fully expect her to have significant academic achievements. Her foster parents believe this accelerated academic progress is because Joanna feels safe to make mistakes and is therefore more likely to push herself beyond her comfort zone.

Whilst the current DME provision is deemed to be strong, there are concerns about the future. The local secondary school is known to be less flexible in relation to personalised provision and there is a history of excluding learners who do not conform to behavioural expectations. Joanna's foster parents are concerned that the secondary school will exclude Joanna when she makes mistakes or cannot cope and they feel that this will be unfair, particularly if it is because the provision was not right at the outset.

The foster parents believe that exclusion in general does not work, as it only passes the problem onto somebody else, causing emotional damage to the child in the process. However, the likelihood is that they will send Joanna to the local secondary school because Joanna herself wants to go there.

If an exclusion were to occur, the foster parents are clear that they would fight this based on the Equality Act and reasonable adjustments, but they hope that it would never come to that. If necessary, the foster parents have said that they would personally remain on-site at the school to ensure that Joanna could stay there. They will do whatever it takes to meet Joanna's needs.

Summary of key learning points

What is the school offer?

The offer at this school has focused heavily on coproduction and on nurturing the High Learning Potential of children with DME. Communication has been open, regular and non-judgemental with a focus on identifying solutions rather than on sanctions for unwanted behaviours. Having regular communication between home and school can be reassuring for all concerned and this is particularly effective when there is a consistent named contact at the school.

What are the strengths of this approach?

The strengths of this approach come through the positive attitude of the school in finding and building upon Joanna's strengths. Why they did this when Joanna's abilities had not been recognised by six schools previously is testimony both to the school and to Joanna's foster carers for believing in her. It is also a testimony to the grit and resilience Joanna has shown in the face of numerous set-backs. The leadership within the school, the belief that her teachers have shown in finding Joanna's strengths and the involvement of all parties in working together as equals should make all of them very proud indeed.

What could have been done differently?

There is little that Joanna's current school has done that should have been done differently. Even recognising that transition may be a problem for Joanna when she goes to secondary school has already been discussed and the issues highlighted so that a strategy can be put in place to minimise any risks. Perhaps the only issue which can be identified is that Joanna had to get to school seven before her needs began to be met.

Key recommendations for schools

1. Ensure that Individual Provision Maps, IEPs (Individual Education Plans) or PEPs (Personalised Education Plans) include provision for the High Learning Potential aspect of children with DME. This may involve the SENCO, the GATCO and a wider pool of professionals.
2. Put structures and processes in place that facilitate regular dialogue between home and school. It is important that these discussions are not just about addressing issues and that they also include the strengths of provision and celebrate positive impact. This will develop stronger relationships so that everybody is better placed to deal with the challenges that will inevitably arise.
3. Take opportunities, particularly as school leaders, to engage in education research to develop a research-informed workforce that delivers evidence-based practice.

Reflection from the authors on effective practice and areas for development/consideration

If there was ever a case study that highlighted the importance of a strengths-based approach to DME then this is it. It is difficult to know which of the elements of the process to highlight first; Joanna's foster carers for highlighting and nurturing her strengths and working with the school to support the development of these; the school for making appropriate and personalised adjustments to their behaviour management process and such frameworks as how they rewarded her effort and attainment; or, indeed, Joanna herself for the resilience she has shown in moving from a child who left six previous schools to one who is beginning to maximise her potential at her current school.

This case study also highlights the impact that coproduction can have on teaching and learning where there is a working partnership between parents/carers, teachers and other professionals and the child or young person themselves.

Finding a secondary school which is able to meet Joanna's needs so well is vital and it is of some concern that the secondary school earmarked for her may not meet all of these. Getting the right support for her through extra-curricular activities will be essential in the future and will make an important contribution towards maintaining and increasing her confidence. With advocates like her foster carers and an advocate or champion within her next school, it is hoped that Joanne will continue to maximise her potential.

Thea's story

Box 5.4

What are her specific strengths? Extremely high levels of ability across the board.

What are her specific needs? Sensory issues, social, emotional and mental health issues.

Schooling: State primary school, home education, primary school.

Introduction to the child and the context

As soon as Thea went into reception class, she said that she felt 'different'. She was extremely perceptive for her age and emotionally mature. However, this feeling of 'difference' was making her miserable. According to her parents, she laid awake for hours at night, feeling anxious and unable to sleep; and repeatedly asked her parents what was wrong with her.

Thea attended reception at the local state primary school, where she was quickly put onto the SEND register at school. Thea's difficulties were seen as 'deficits' and her social needs were regarded as being due to communication difficulties.

However, Thea's parents saw a child who communicated well with older children and adults. She was also a child who thrived with a combination of challenge and careful support. This support enabled her to access more complex problems and then, with the right encouragement, she was even more willing to go out of her 'comfort zone' and attempt things that she found more difficult such as physical activities.

Her parents also recognised that Thea was highly sensitive, not only emotionally but also physically. She was easily overwhelmed, and it was felt by her parents that this was clouding the school's judgement of her actual academic ability.

Identification of DME

As Thea became increasingly withdrawn and isolated, her parents wanted more information and approached the charity Potential Plus UK. After several calls with an educational adviser, they decided to have Thea assessed so that they could understand her learning profile – her relative strengths and weaknesses – and so that they and the school could provide her with more appropriate support.

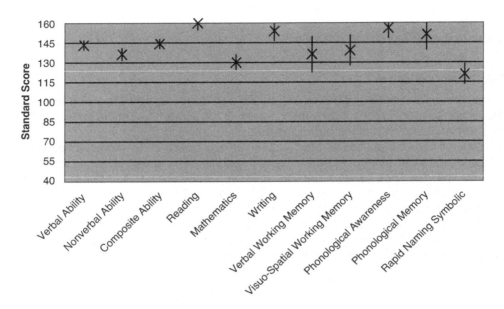

Figure 5.3

In the assessment, Thea scored exceptionally highly on both the verbal and nonverbal sections of the assessment. She demonstrated cognitive functioning on the 99.8th percentile (a rarity of 1 in 500 people) and her attainment was on the 99.9th percentile (1 in 1,000) when she was given the opportunity to attempt more difficult concepts in a safe environment.

An accompanying sensory profile highlighted that she had sensory issues in several areas including auditory and visual sensitivities which would continue to impact upon her achievement and well-being if not addressed.

Description of DME provision

Unfortunately, the school Thea attended at the time did not take on board the recommendations in the assessment report. As a result, and reluctantly, Thea's parents took the difficult decision to withdraw her from formal schooling for a period whilst they looked for alternative provision. Now that they had more information about Thea's strengths and the challenges she faced, they were able to find a school which was receptive to working with them.

The school to which Thea moved was receptive to many of the assessment report's recommendations which included providing an accelerated academic curriculum in Thea's areas of strength; working collaboratively with a local secondary school as time progressed; and providing opportunities for Thea to work on non-academic issues of social interest. To help meet her challenges, Thea had an integrated support plan for her auditory and visual needs.

All of this was brought together and co-ordinated by the SENCO via an IEP which ensured a formal framework for action and a process which could be regularly monitored and evaluated.

Impact of DME provision

The combination of an appropriate level of challenge with peers of a similar ability and opportunities for self-directed study, along with adaptations for her heightened sensory issues, have enabled Thea to better manage her anxieties and develop her self-identity.

The school has also benefited from its understanding of the needs of DME learners and the support provided to them through organisations such as Potential Plus UK. This has enabled them to identify and put in appropriate provision for other DME learners in their setting.

Thea's parents recognise that they will need to navigate the 'rollercoaster of having a child with DME', especially during transition in school and between schools. Both they and the school acknowledge that the collaborative nature of their relationship has been crucial to ensuring Thea's well-being so far.

Summary of key learning points

What is the school offer?

The school was open-minded about what it needed to do to support Thea and recognised that, to address her sensory issues within the context of an ability they might only see in 1 in 500 children, they might need to think out of the box.

Their offer for her was an accelerated academic curriculum in Thea's areas of strength; giving her opportunities to work collaboratively with a local secondary school as time progressed, and opportunities for Thea to work on non-academic issues of social interest. All of this could be accommodated within the existing school timetable, although careful liaison needed to take place with others such as the secondary school.

Once this was in place, Thea's Special Educational Needs could be accommodated like any other child with SEND and the school was confident about doing this. The IEP helped to ensure that there was a framework and clear structure in place to monitor and evaluate this provision.

What are the strengths of this approach?

Even though Thea's Special Educational Needs had been recognised, her abilities might have gone unsupported and this might have carried on if her parents had not paid for the assessment and evaluation to take place. The school chosen by Thea and her parents was ultimately open to the challenge they faced and was prepared to work collaboratively to devise a programme which could be accommodated with the existing school timetable. Once this had happened, supporting Thea's Special Educational Needs became easy and the rest could be incorporated within the school's SEND structure. Key strengths therefore of the approach were that the school was open-minded and collaborative; they knew when there was a role for external organisations, when they could handle provision themselves and that they were prepared to meet the challenge of a situation they would not have encountered many times before and 'think outside the box'

What could have been done differently?

It is a pity that the first school felt unable to make the accommodations required to support Thea. Notwithstanding, it would have been useful, particularly in these times of scarce resources within schools, for them to be clear about what they were and were not able to accommodate to enable Thea's parents to make their decision accordingly. This would have meant that Thea's parents could have searched sooner for a new school and this would have caused less stress and anxiety.

That said, Thea's current school seems to have approached the issue pragmatically, knowing what they can fit into current timetables and what they can handle themselves, and they would be a good role model for other schools.

The key challenge will be when Thea transitions to secondary school, both in finding a school able to meet her DME and in putting in place provision within the school curriculum to meet it.

Key recommendations for schools

1. Be open and honest about what can (and cannot) be delivered to support a child's DME.
2. See the value of collaboration with parents/carers and child or young person to meet the needs of the DME pupil.
3. Build on the strengths of the child or young person and use these to support the challenges they face.
4. Know when to bring in external organisations and when the skills and structures are available internally to support the needs of the child or young person with DME.

5. Where possible, accommodate support for the child or young person with DME into existing structures and timetables.
6. Bring together people who can 'think outside the box'.

Reflection from the authors on effective practice and areas for development/ consideration

It is not expected that schools, certainly at primary school level, will often see a case like Thea's. Notwithstanding, the elements of this case study will be similar no matter how high the individual's ability.

Other children may exhibit other forms of behaviour which mask their High Learning Potential and teachers need to keep an open mind and observe whether DME issues are at the root of these. Supporting DME need not be difficult and can almost always be accommodated into the existing school curriculum with imagination, thinking out of the box and a willingness to look at alternative solutions in partnership with others internally or external to the school.

Jamie's story

Box 5.5

What are his specific strengths? General high ability.

What are his specific needs? Autistic Spectrum Condition, Emotional Behavioural Disorder (EBD), anxiety, low confidence and self-esteem, social phobia and agoraphobia.

Schooling: Home education with home tuition service, home education with Nisai Learning (see appendices for more information), secondary school.

Introduction to the child and the context

Jamie stopped going to school when he was 10 years old because of a variety of different issues including Autism Spectrum Condition and EBD. The home tuition service of the local authority had been trying to engage him in education and had been sending tutors into his home for over three years. However, there had been little success with this and over the years Jamie had developed low confidence and self-esteem, severe anxiety, social phobia and finally agoraphobia. All of this meant that Jamie did not leave his bedroom and had become an elective mute. This made educating him extremely difficult, even though he was bright.

Engaging with Jamie and providing him with a worthwhile education had become extremely complicated. He would knock on his bedroom door to communicate; once for yes and twice for no. He would also pass messages under the door but would have no face-to-face interaction with the tutors sent in to provide his education. This was worrying and of concern to everyone involved.

Identification of DME

Finally, the home tuition service referred the case back to Jamie's school. They recommended that the school should speak to an organisation called Nisai Learning regarding his education.

Nisai Learning was established in 1997 to provide flexible, innovative education programmes which support learners up to the age of 25, creating pathways to their further learning and employment. They specialise in providing tailored programmes for individuals, including those with DME, who need to access education through non-traditional routes. This includes those who, for one reason or another, need to be educated at home, within mainstream school offering separate programmes and within schools which specialise in non-traditional learning. A core element of the approach is online learning, which is tailored to the strengths and challenges of the individual learner.

Given the experience of, and on the recommendation of, the local authority's home tuition service, it was suggested that the school and Nisai Learning should develop an online learning programme for Jamie, being taught in the first instance at home for the remainder of the academic Year 10. Based on the results of this initial one-term trial, it was agreed that, if successful, this could be extended for a further year.

Jamie started a customised online education programme with Nisai Learning when he was 14 years old. It began with baseline screening carried out by the Nisai team. This showed that he had HLP. Normally, this would have meant that Jamie would have begun his online learning programme at an advanced level. However, as he had effectively missed out on three-and-a-half years of education, the school wanted Nisai to focus on functional skills rather than GCSEs, due to possible gaps in his learning.

Description of DME provision

In the first instance, given the context of the situation, it was agreed that online learning only would be provided.

In terms of his engagement with the programme, Jamie started by using only the private chat function of his learning programme, but progressed quickly onto public chat. He contributed within lessons and began communicating with his peers and this made a major contribution towards building his self-confidence and self-esteem. Over the course of the summer holidays, Jamie used Nisai's live chat function to see what was happening with his education from September. The school finally confirmed his continuation with the programme and he carried on with his functional skills at Level 2 in numeracy and literacy.

Jamie's re-engagement with learning spurred him on and, despite having been out of formal education from the first half-term in Year 7 to Easter in Year 10, his experiences encouraged Jamie to go back in to school, as he had decided that he wanted to become a vet and wouldn't be able to achieve this on the basis of two functional skills. The school agreed that he could return to school and he went back after the October half-term. The immediate response from the teaching staff was that he would affect the class targets.

What no one had known, was that despite appearances that Jamie did not want to engage in education, he had been self-learning from his bedroom during the time he had been absent from school. Therefore, when the school assessed him, they found that Jamie was working at As and Bs across the board at GCSE level. The use of online learning had provided him with structure, the exposure to a classroom environment and interaction with his peers which helped to re-energize his education.

Impact of DME provision

Following his return, Jamie never missed a day of school in Year 11 and achieved seven GCSEs at B and above. In addition, his growing confidence helped to gain him a small but trusted group of friends at school, which he hadn't had earlier and which wouldn't have been possible before Nisai Learning had helped him to get him back to school.

Summary of key learning points

What is the school offer?

This case study outlines a situation where the school needed to explore non-traditional approaches to learning. This young person had been out of a formal school environment for over six years and some of the difficulties associated with his disabilities and Special Educational Needs had been exacerbated by mental health problems, including lack of self-esteem, social anxiety and phobia. The school involved was not prepared to write off this pupil but to work positively with another organisation to seek Jamie's long-term re-integration back into the traditional school environment. This took courage by the school and a commitment that no child or young person would be left behind. Although this approach cost the school money, the net benefit of the approach at this time for this young person in terms of the results achieved far outweighed the costs both of the alternatives which had not worked and in terms of what might have happened to Jamie in the future if he had not gone back to school.

What are the strengths of this approach?

This approach began with the individual and developed a customised approach to their learning needs, recognising that someone who did not talk or engage with others at all or leave their bedroom might need a level of support, in this instance delivered through online learning. This was successful because it focused on their educational needs but also included issues, such as engaging with other students, which the individual found difficult. As a young person who had DME, the motivation to learn for themselves, particularly in areas of interest, was strong; but it took a formal intervention delivered in a non-traditional way, along with support for other issues, to achieve what years of home education could not.

What could have been done differently?

The school was concerned about giving Jamie the functional skills he required following such a gap in his education. This is understandable. Notwithstanding, once Nisai Learning had conducted its baseline assessment which showed that he was a DME pupil, this should have been recognised. Therefore, parallel to the functional skills learning provided, a programme of higher-level education should also have been implemented. This may have increased Jamie's motivation to evaluate sooner his plans for his future learning and earlier return to school.

Key recommendations for schools

1. Keep an open mind on the efficacy of different schooling methods which go beyond the traditional for some children and young people.
2. Build on the holistic needs of the child with DME to ensure that both their education needs and their social, emotional and psychological needs are taken into consideration in any learning programme.
3. Explore all of the different approaches on offer to ensure that children and young people engage with their learning. This includes non-traditional solutions where they are needed.
4. Have the courage to implement a range of learning options for DME and other children who are the hardest to reach. Within resource levels, do not be afraid to pilot such programmes and evaluate their success.

Reflection from the authors on effective practice and areas for development/consideration

With the growth in exclusion and self-exclusion, the increase in home education and other difficulties associated with engagement in traditional schooling methods, alternative learning approaches for some pupils, including those with DME, need to be found. Nisai Learning offers a child-centred, customised approach which has online learning at its core, and which can be used both to teach and to encourage children and young people to re-engage with schooling in both the short- and long-term. This approach should certainly be considered by schools as part of their overall strategy for DME.

Alex's story

Box 5.6

What are his specific strengths? High ability in music and drama and the creative arts.

What are his specific needs? Dyslexia, dysgraphia, dyscalculia, anxiety, issues with working memory.

Schooling: Private nursery, state primary school, state secondary school and sixth form leading to drama school.

Introduction to the child and the context

Alex was a highly verbal child; speaking in whole sentences by the age of 2. By 3 he could tell his family members stories which tapped into his vivid imagination and which left them in no doubt what a bright boy they had. He went to a local private nursery setting on a part-time basis and they confirmed what his parents had thought when his key worker talked to them about his intellectual boredom being a possible reason for the sudden onset of his misbehaviour. His key worker recommended that he should be moved to primary school as soon as possible to get greater intellectual stimulation, which his parents did.

At school, he enjoyed anything which enabled him to talk and use his imagination. However, he struggled at the outset with his handwriting and organisational skills and avoided reading wherever possible. His maths ability was also extremely variable. For example, he struggled with mental maths, but he was extremely good at anything which involved visual or spatial maths.

His teachers could not understand how that when he was asked a question, he usually knew the answer. However, when he had to write anything down or concentrate on something in which he wasn't interested, he did not engage. Various teachers put it down to everything from laziness to poor behaviour to lack of ability.

As he grew older, Alex became the class clown and was good at playing his teachers and parents off against each other to get out of homework which, when he had to do it, was a nightmare at home and could take the better part of a day to complete. His parents found that if he dictated it to them it was fine and then they dictated it back to him in 'chunks' over the course of the day. Sometimes this lasted into the evening as he grew tired quickly and found it difficult to write for long periods.

By the time he was 8, his parents were extremely worried about Alex. They began to research everything about various Special Educational Needs, looking for answers about what was going on in school. He could read when he set his mind to it, although he wasn't a natural reader, and so dyslexia didn't cross anyone's mind. In addition, providing maths was explained visually or spatially, his only issues seemed to be with lack of interest and ability to process information. Lack of organisational skills was still a problem but that was ut down to it just 'being Alex'.

In secondary school, Alex remained the class clown and his parents were regularly contacted by his teachers 'because of his sense of humour' and imaginative antics. However, what they didn't realise until many years later was that he was also bullied by the other boys because he did not like things like football, preferring music and drama.

To build on his strengths and his interests, his parents paid for music lessons and a drama club in the local community and these were recognised when he was placed on the 'Gifted and Talented Register' at school. This amused Alex because, from the age of about 8 or 9 his self-esteem in terms of his schoolwork had been rapidly decreasing, making school in most cases a negative experience for him. For example, when asked who was better than he was at maths he answered, 'an ant'.

Identification of the DME

After years of struggling to find answers, when he was about 13, his parents finally took him to be assessed privately with an educational psychologist specialising in High Learning Potential and Special Educational Needs. He identified Alex's high verbal ability and visuo-spatial strengths and also his poor processing speeds and reading, writing and maths issues. He suggested that dyslexia and dysgraphia might be the cause of his issues and recommended various accommodations to be made in the classroom, including increased time in exams and use of new technology, as well as support for his dysgraphia.

His parents quizzed the psychologist about his dyslexia and specifically his reading, which hadn't been spotted by anyone, including them. They were told that Alex's brain was filling in the missing letters and reorganising the jumble so that he could read.

Description of DME provision

Alex's parents took the psychologist's report into school and their first experiences of the SENCO and his form teacher were negative. The SENCO said that they didn't have a support programme 'at a high enough level' for Alex. His form teacher and Head of Year said they were surprised at the results and 'would have treated Alex differently if they had known'. They had all thought he was badly behaved and a lazy pupil. It took a change of SENCO and a new form tutor for the situation to change.

Alex was then given support from the Special Educational Needs Department to help him with his organisational skills and support during exams including additional time and access to a computer. He took the higher paper in GCSE maths where he could get more marks for his areas of strengths. He had repeatedly struggled with the lower paper as he was not as good at simple mathematical calculations. Having failed to secure his GCSE maths at aged 16, special dispensation allowed him to enter the sixth form without this qualification. Subsequently, with additional support, he passed his GCSE maths exam when he was aged 17. His Headteacher shook his hand on the day that he got his results and, even though he got a C, he said how proud he was of the result given how much Alex had struggled. Alex said that he felt so proud that day.

He took a course within the community, paid for by his parents, where he learnt to write again from scratch, how to sit, how to hold his pen, how to position his chair and paper and the tutor gave him a style of writing whereby it was easier for him to write given that they had identified problems with hypermobility. All of this was successful in helping to ensure that his handwriting was legible, albeit a little slow.

The reason why he struggled with reading was also explored through various eye tests and reading exercises where it was discovered that his eyes jumped from one line to the other, which meant that he read the same line numerous times. He also struggled with different coloured printed paper in books. He was told to stick to certain colours and use a ruler or sheet to keep to the same line. A pair of glasses also helped with this problem, although for some variants of scotopic sensitivity syndrome, more specialist provision may be required.

However, the biggest impact on his work came from the provision of a mentor who he trusted and respected and to whom he could go to discuss any problems he was facing.

This person also helped to give him the confidence to build on his strengths and to see what he was good at. Thus, when he failed his English Literature GCSE and could not take the A level – something he had wanted to do – his mentor helped him to see that this was not a disaster but instead encouraged him to take Dance A level and use it as an opportunity for the future.

At the same time as bolstering his Special Educational Needs, the school made sure that his talents gave him the skills and confidence both to believe in himself and to enable him to do the 'hard stuff'. Building on the advice of his mentor, he deliberately took A levels which built on these strengths; in dance, music and drama. All of these were practical subjects which built upon his imagination, sense of performance and visuo-spatial strengths. The school recommended that he should do these three subjects rather than additional A levels so that he didn't become too overwhelmed, particularly because of his difficulties with organisation skills and his subsequent anxiety. He got his A levels because of his strengths rather than his written ability, balancing top grades in performance with low marks in his written work.

During all of this, particularly in later secondary school and sixth form, his parents and the school worked closely together. The school had an open-door policy and parents could meet with key staff, including his mentor, when they had an issue. The school also knew that they could phone his parents if there was a problem, for example, failing to hand course work in on time. This positive relationship was built on mutual respect and this enabled constructive problem-solving to take place. Wherever possible, Alex was built into these meetings so that his views could be considered and, wherever possible, acted upon.

He was encouraged to apply for drama school, even though the process is hard with a low success rate, and he got into one of the country's leading schools. One of the first questions his group was asked when it started the course was 'how many people have dyslexia?' A number of other students raised their hands and Alex felt that the course he did understood and supported these needs. This included having lectures recorded so that he could watch them again and again or in small sections, and keeping writing to a minimum as well as giving people plenty of time to get work done. He also felt that, for the first time, he was taught to understand exam questions and how to structure his answers in a way that he understood.

Impact of DME provision

Alex is now training to be an actor and is on track to get a top grade at the end of his studies, including for some of his written work, which he has been motivated to do within time limits which have not put him at a disadvantage because of his written ability and lower processing speeds (as in exams). He never used a laptop for his exams at school because it made him appear 'different' but using a laptop for his written work at drama school really helped.

His aim is to succeed in the industry and his ambition now is to join the Royal Shakespeare Company (RSC). He could not have done any of this without his secondary school and his mentor and their belief that he was more than just the class clown with the quirky imagination and sense of humour.

Summary of key learning points

What is the school offer?

Provision was very much built into the day-to-day timetable of the school. This can be important, particularly at secondary age, as many young people do not want to stand out or 'appear different'. For example, until Alex saw that many of his friends were going to the support group for Special Educational Needs he would not attend. He also refused a laptop because it would make him appear 'different' from the other pupils during exams.

What are the strengths of this approach?

The school built on the strengths of the pupil and used these to motivate and give him confidence rather than first using an approach to 'address and support' his Special Educational Needs. In addition, the school had an open-door policy, welcomed his parent's input and listened to their concerns and views.

What could have been done differently?

Although nursery and secondary school recognised Alex's strengths, the lack of recognition in particular at his primary school that he could be both bright and have a special need caused Alex's self-confidence to reduce significantly. This also happened in early secondary school. Whilst it is recognised that many teachers want their pupils to start each new year or school with a 'clean slate', passing on information from one to the other would have been useful, as there were some subjects Alex struggled with and no information had been passed to the teacher about how best to support him. Also, a positive attitude by the SENCO was essential to enable Alex's Special Educational Needs and abilities to be recognised and supported in the right way. Therefore, providing key staff with the skills to develop appropriate work and tailored support programmes and to recognise the needs of a child or young person with both SEND and HLP is important and may need to be delivered through training and staff development.

Key recommendations for schools

1. Carry out an accurate assessment and identification as early as possible of a child or young person who may be DME. This will prevent an escalation of issues as they progress through school.
2. Build on the strengths of the child and use these to address areas of special need.

3. Ensure there is greater awareness of DME in schools and with parents/carers so that the signs of DME in the classroom and at home can be spotted and appropriately supported.
4. Consider merging SEND and HLP provision and calling it inclusion.
5. Consider appointing mentors for all pupils who need them.

Reflection from the authors on effective practice and areas for development/consideration

This is an excellent example of how a school can meet the needs of DME pupils through existing provision. The passion of individual teachers along with their understanding about how to get the best from each child or young person is at the core of this story, along with a partnership between the SENCO and those responsible for HLP to ensure all pupils achieve to the best of their abilities. Developing school-wide strategies for inclusion will enable the needs of both groups of children to be effectively recognised, and whilst this would take a policy decision on behalf of the school (perhaps driven by national government support) it can be done within existing resources and provision.

Recommendations arising from the stories

Although these stories provide a snap-shot of a small number of children at specific points in time, many of the issues raised can be applied to DME on three different levels within a) national government and by policymakers, b) a whole-school approach and c) classroom provision, and in terms of what should be done to improve support for DME children and young people.

Recommendations for national governments and policymakers

1. Recognise the importance of DME as a national issue within education and raise awareness of DME within policy documents, within the school system and elsewhere such as within alternative provision, the care system and the youth offending system.
2. Appoint a national DME Champion who can advocate for the needs of children with DME across the country.
3. Build DME identification and provision into initial teacher education and other training programmes where children with DME can be found.
4. Engage school leaders in education research, so that they can develop a research-informed workforce that delivers evidence-based practice and can inform the development of national good practice on DME.
5. Commission further research work on DME and use this to develop leading edge practice in this field.

Recommendations for a whole-school approach

Culture and values:

1. Ensure that school leaders and governors support effective DME provision through all elements of the ethos and culture of the school. For example, zero-tolerance approaches to managing behaviour may be incompatible with inclusion and personalised provision.
2. Be open-minded in working with parents/carers and children and young people on coproduction.
3. Have the courage and ethical leadership to implement a range of learning options for learners with DME and for other children who are the hardest to reach. Within resource constraints, do not be afraid to pilot innovative programmes and evaluate their success.
4. Keep an open mind on the efficacy of different schooling methods which go beyond the traditional for some children and young people.

Strategy and policy:

1. Develop a school-wide strategy to raise awareness of DME amongst school staff, parents/carers and pupils to identify and support learners with DME as part of an inclusion strategy.
2. Ensure that there is a school-wide DME policy in place, which will help to create a consistent approach to the identification of DME.
3. Consider merging HLP and SEND provision as part of a holistic inclusion strategy within the school.
4. Recognise that transition between schools, but also between one class and the next, can be difficult for DME pupils and put in place a school-wide strategy to support them and other pupils with this.
5. Establish a school-wide mentoring programme to support DME and other pupils who need support in this way. Mentors could be drawn from the staff, or could be older pupils with experience of DME, parents, carers or other volunteers.

Supporting DME:

1. Appoint a school-wide DME Champion to advocate for and support the needs of DME pupils within the school. This could be a particular teacher, senior leader, governor or trustee who is passionate about DME.
2. Involve a range of professionals and others (such as parents, carers and young people) to identify both the needs and strengths of children and young people with DME and to input into the shaping of provision and the development of a school-wide strategy.
3. Ensure that Individual Provision Maps, IEPs or PEPs include provision for the High Learning Potential aspect of children with DME. This may involve the SENCO, the GATCO and a wider pool of professionals.
4. Encourage groups of children and young people across the school to work together in key interest areas.

Recommendations for classroom provision

Awareness:

1. Be aware of, seek to understand and believe in DME and how it can be supported in the classroom.
2. Be aware that the responses of the child or young person towards their DME may change over time and be flexible in meeting these needs.
3. Be aware that the characteristics and behaviours of the child might be different at home and at school. Share information and understanding about this with parents and carers and use it to help shape practice in the classroom.

Working with families:

1. See the value of collaboration with a parent/carer or child or young person (as appropriate) to meet the needs of a pupil with DME.
2. Keep an open mind about the information which parents/carers provide and an open door which gives them access, without concern, to exploring what they know.
3. Pool knowledge with parents and carers to get the best outcomes for the child or young person with DME.
4. Have the confidence to tell parents and carers when you are not familiar with an issue so that you can learn from them and others.
5. Be open and honest about what you can (and cannot) deliver to support a child's DME.
6. Put structures and processes in place that facilitate regular dialogue between home and school. It is important that these discussions are not just about addressing issues but that they also include the strengths of provision and celebrate positive impact. This will develop stronger relationships so that everybody is better placed to deal with the challenges that will inevitably arise.

Supporting learners:

1. Where possible, accommodate support for the child or young person with DME into existing structures and timetables. Where this is not possible, explore all of the different approaches on offer to ensure that children and young people can engage with their learning. This includes non-traditional solutions where they are needed.
2. Know when to bring in external organisations and when you have the skills and structures internally to support the needs of a learner with DME.
3. Do not be afraid to bring together people who can 'think outside the box' on an issue regarding a child with DME.
4. Carry out accurate assessment and identification as early as possible of a child or young person who may be DME. This will prevent an escalation of issues as they progress through school.
5. Build on the strengths of the child or young person and use these to address their Special Educational Needs. This could be through work which builds on their strengths e.g. in terms of subject material or in terms of how it is produced such as the use of new technology.
6. Build on the holistic needs of the child with DME to ensure that both their education needs and their social, emotional and psychological needs are taken into consideration in any learning programme.

Whilst different issues will come to the fore with different children, these key suggestions can help to provide a blueprint for supporting children and young people with DME.

Box 5.7 Ten myths of supporting pupils with DME

Myth No. 9: Pupils with DME can't have EHC plans or IEPs or the equivalent.

Some schools believe that, because a child or young person appears to meet the year targets, they are doing 'all right' and do not require an IEP, EHC plan or the equivalent. This is not true. Best practice in supporting children with DME suggests that a framework to ensure both their Special Educational Needs or Disabilities and their HLP should be put in place. This will help to ensure that all parties – professional staff, parents and carers and the children and young people themselves – can focus both on the strengths and issues facing the pupil and also that there is an understanding that both are interrelated and must be seen together. Simply put, when the child's ability is supported, their Special Educational Needs have a better chance of being met.

Myth No. 10: It would require too many resources to provide for learners with DME at the same time as everyone else.

This is not true. Every school will have a strategy and approach to support its pupils with SEND. Good practice dictates that every school should also have a strategy and approach to support its HLP (gifted and talented and more able) pupils. All that is needed is to put the two together in the context of a strengths-based approach for children with DME. Elements required include:

- Understanding and 'buy-in' of DME from the governors and senior leadership team.
- Understanding and 'buy-in' from both the SEND team and the team responsible for HLP. This could include training on things like the identification of these children and the challenge and support which can be provided. Many schools have already taken a step towards this by merging SEND and gifted and talented into an overall inclusion strategy which nurtures the potential of all its pupils, no matter what their abilities.
- Training for key professionals, which could include classroom teachers, teaching or learning support assistants and others who might come into contact with children and young people with DME, including lunchtime supervisors.

None of this will require any additional resources beyond what a school will already be doing.

Conclusion
The way forward for DME in your school

Children and young people with DME can be found in every school and in every area of the country. For many years the very existence of these pupils has been ignored and they have been labelled as lazy, badly behaved underachievers. We believe that without recognition and the right support, many of these children and young people are dropping out of school, whether by being excluded or self-excluding, with a subsequent risk of offending behaviour, mental health issues or worse.

The fundamental question which you need to consider as a school, a teacher, a SENCO or a GATCO is what are you going to do to help these children to achieve their capabilities?

This book is the first step towards bringing DME back onto the education policy agenda in the UK. We recognise that more work needs to be done to identify and build on the good practice that is already going on in schools now to make sure that other schools can learn from this. We also recognise that further research into different aspects of DME is needed.

However, we hope that every school, including yours, will explore Dual and Multiple Exceptionality seriously as an issue and will begin by raising awareness and developing appropriate strategies to support these children. Their future is, literally, in your hands.

References

Abrams, F. (2019) Grammar School Expansion Still Locking Out the Poor. *Guardian article: 26th February 2019*. www.theguardian.com/education/2019/feb/26/grammar-school-expansion-still-locking-out-the-poor Accessed in August 2019.

Bartram, D. and Patel, V. (2016) SEND Review Guide: A School-Led Approach to Improving Provision for All. *Crown Copyright*. www.sendgateway.org.uk/download.B034695A-65E1-4E5B-9A91D6C1DDAEBEE8.html Accessed in July 2019.

Boddison, A. (2019) Perspectives from the SEND Sector: nasen. www.goodcareerguidance.org.uk/send/nasen Accessed in September 2019.

Boyle, D. and Harris, M. (2009) The Challenge of Coproduction: How Equal Partnerships between Professionals and the Public are Crucial to Improving Public Services. Nesta discussion paper available from: https://media.nesta.org.uk/documents/the_challenge_of_co-production.pdf Accessed in September 2019.

Casey, R. and Koshy, V. (2013) Gifted and Talented Education: The English Policy Highway at a Crossroads. *Journal for the Education of the Gifted*, Vol. 36, no. 1, pp. 44–65.

Curran, H., Maloney, H., Heavey, A. and Boddison, A. (2018) It's about Time: The Impact of SENCO Workload on the Professional and the School. www.bathspa.ac.uk/media/bathspaacuk/education-/research/senco-workload/SENCOWorkloadReport-FINAL2018.pdf Accessed in June 2019.

DCSF. (2008) Identifying Gifted and Talented Learners: Getting Started. *Department for Children, Schools and Families*. webarchive.nationalarchives.gov.uk/20110907134700/www.education.gov.uk/publications/eOrderingDownload/Getting%20StartedWR.pdf Accessed in September 2019.

DfE. (2008) Gifted and Talented Education: Helping to Find and Support Children with Dual or Multiple Exceptionalities. Published as part of the National Strategies for the Department for Education. Crown Copyright. webarchive.nationalarchives.gov.uk/20130323073730/www.education.gov.uk/publications/eOrderingDownload/00052-2008BKT-EN.pdf Accessed in August 2019.

DfE. (2019a) Special Education Needs in England: National Statistics January 2019. *Department for Education*. www.gov.uk/government/statistics/special-educational-needs-in-england-january-2019 Accessed in August 2019.

DfE. (2019b) Governance Handbook: For Academies, Multi-Academy Trusts and Maintained Schools. Published by the Department for Education, March 2019. https://assets.publishing.service.gov.uk/government/uploads/system/uploads/attachment_data/file/788234/governance_handbook_2019.pdf Accessed in September 2019.

DfE and DoH. (2015) Special Educational Needs Code of Practice: 0–25 Years. Statutory Guidance for Organisations Which Work with and Support Children and Young People Who Have Special Educational Needs or Disabilities. *Health*. https://assets.publishing.service.gov.uk/government/uploads/system/uploads/attachment_data/file/398815/SEND_Code_of_Practice_January_2015.pdf Accessed in September 2019.

Education Scotland. (2019) Parentzone. website: https://education.gov.scot/parentzone/additional-support/What%20are%20additional%20support%20needs Accessed in September 2019.

Foster, D. and Danechi, S. (2019) Home Education in England. House of Commons Briefing Paper 5108.

Fox, J. (2009) *How to Discover and Develop Your Child's Strengths: A Guide for Parents and Teachers*. London: Penguin books.

Freeman, J. (1998) *Educating the Very Able: Current International Research*. London: The Stationery Office. www.joanfreeman.com/pdf/Ofsted-report-final-text-Feb-98.pdf Accessed in September 2019.

Godfrey, D., Seleznyov, S., Anders, J., Wollaston, N. and Barrera-Pedemonte, F. (2017) A Developmental Evaluation Approach to Lesson Study: Exploring the Impact of Lesson Study in London Schools. *Professional Development in Education*, Vol. 45, no. 2, pp. 325–340.

Longfield, A. (2019) in Hinds, D. (2019) New Register to Help All Children Get the Education They Deserve. Department for Education press release, 2nd April 2019. www.gov.uk/government/news/new-register-to-help-all-children-get-the-education-they-deserve Accessed in September 2019.

Ming Cheung, W. and Yee Wong, W. (2014) Does Lesson Study Work? *International Journal for Lesson and Learning Studies*, Vol. 3, no. 2, pp. 137–149.

MoJ. (2019) Youth Justice Statistics 2017–18 for England and Wales. *Youth Justice Board and Ministry of Justice January 2019.* www.gov.uk/government/statistics/youth-justice-statistics-2017-to-2018 Accessed in July 2019.

Montgomery, D. (2015) *Teaching Gifted Children with Special Educational Needs: Supporting Dual and Multiple Exceptionality.* London: Routledge.

Mouchel. (2005) National Quality Standards in Gifted and Talented Education. www.egfl.org.uk/sites/default/files/Services_for_children/National_Quality_Standards_in_GT_Education.pdf   Accessed   in September 2019.

NAGC. (2012) Releasing Potential. High Learning Potential in the Youth Justice System. National Association for Gifted Children (now Potential Plus UK) March 2012. www.potentialplusuk.org/wp-content/uploads/2016/08/Releasing-Potential-Executive-Summary-leaflet.pdf Accessed in June 2019.

nasen. (2016) Girls and Autism: Flying under the Radar. A nasen Miniguide. www.nasen.org.uk/resources/resources.girls-and-autism-flying-under-the-radar.html Accessed in September 2019.

NGA. (2019) Eight Elements of Effective Governance. National Governance Association website article. www.nga.org.uk/Knowledge-Centre/Good-governance/Effective-governance/Eight-Elements-of-Effective-Governance.aspx Accessed in September 2019.

Ofsted. (2019) Education Inspection Framework (EIF). www.gov.uk/government/publications/education-inspection-framework Accessed in August 2019.

Poortvliet, M., Axford, N. and Lloyd, J. (2018) Working with Parents to Support Children's Learning. Guidance Report published by the Education Endowment Foundation. https://educationendowmentfoundation.org.uk/public/files/Publications/ParentalEngagement/EEF_Parental_Engagement_Guidance_Report.pdf Accessed in September 2019.

Potential Plus UK. (2015) Raise the Bar and Mind the Gap. www.potentialplusuk.org/wp-content/uploads/2017/06/Manifesto-2015.pdf Accessed in July 2019.

Potential Plus UK. (2018) Advice Sheet on High Learning Potential. www.potentialplusuk.org/wp-content/uploads/2018/06/S00-High-Learning-Potential-180618.pdf Accessed in September 2019.

Purdy, N. and Boddison, A. (2018) Special Educational Needs and Inclusion. In Cremin, T. and Burnett, C. (eds.) *Learning to Teach in the Primary School.* London: Routledge.

Ryan, A. and Waterman, C. (2018) Dual and Multiple Exceptionality: The Current State of Play. www.nasen.org.uk/utilities/download.5ED13CB8-C8CD-4598-AF82808652F25719.html Accessed in September 2019.

Silverman, L. (2007) *What We Have Learned about Gifted Children 1979–2007.* Gifted Development Center.

Silverman, L. (2013) *Giftedness 101.* New York: Springer.

Timpson, E. (2019) The Timpson Review of School Exclusion. Crown Copyright.

Tuffin, R. (2019) Number of Home-Schooled Children in Kent Doubles in Seven Years. KentOnline News article: 25th March 2019. www.kentonline.co.uk/sheerness/news/number-of-homeschooled-children-doubles-201354/ Accessed in September 2019.

Wallace, B., Leydon, S., Montgomery, D., Winstanley, C., Pomerantz, M. and Fitton, S. (2010) *Raising the Achievement of All Pupils within an Inclusive Setting: Practical Strategies for Developing Best Practice.* London: Routledge.

Whittaker, F. (2018) £18m 'Future Talent Fund' Cancelled Less than a Year after It Was Announced. *Schools Week* article: 12th September 2018. https://schoolsweek.co.uk/18m-future-talent-fund-cancelled-less-than-a-year-after-it-was-announced/ Accessed in August 2019.

Williams, S. (2018) School Is Very Oppressive: Why Home-Schooling Is on the Rise. *Guardian* article: 3rd November 2018. www.theguardian.com/education/2018/nov/03/get-to-be-free-rise-in-home-schooling Accessed in August 2019.

Appendix 1

Glossary of terms used

2e – Twice Exceptional. Another term for DME.

ADHD – Attention Deficit Hyperactivity Disorder. this is a behavioural disorder that includes symptoms such as inattentiveness, hyperactivity and impulsiveness.

CAMHS – Children and Adolescent Mental Health Service.

Comorbidity – this is where one or more conditions occur at the same time as the primary condition but with separate characteristics. Usually refers to SEND.

Coproduction – this is where public services are delivered in an equal and reciprocal relationship between professionals, people using the services, families and others in the community.

CRM – Customer Relationship Management system. A database that could be used in schools to log observations and aid triangulation.

Dual and Multiple Exceptional or DME – when a person has one or more Special Educational Needs or Disabilities as well as having High Learning Potential.

EBD – Emotional Behavioural Disorder (often referred to as 'Emotional and Behavioural Difficulties') refers to a condition in which behaviour or emotional responses of an individual are so different from generally accepted norms, that they adversely affect that child's performance.

EHC Plans – Education, Health and Care Plans. Plans which provide a framework to support the holistic needs of a child or young person with SEND in education. Previously called statements of special educational needs.

GATCO – Gifted and Talented Co-ordinator. Sometimes shortened to G&T Co-ordinator. One of the terms used for the teacher responsible for co-ordinating HLP strategy in a school.

G&T – gifted and talented. Another term for HLP still popular in many schools to define children with one or more gifts or talents.

GCSE – General Certificate of Education. Exam normally done in the UK when the young person is in Year 11.

GLD – Gifted with a Learning Disability (sometimes referred to as Gifted with Learning Difficulties). Another term for DME in some countries (e.g. Australia).

Head of Inclusion – person responsible for co-ordinating work on both SEND and HLP into an inclusive school strategy.

HI – hearing impairment.

HLP – High Learning Potential. When a person has abilities in one or more areas or has the potential to show these abilities with the right support. Includes both academic subjects and a range of other areas such as music, art, drama.

IEP – Individual Education Plan. A non-statutory document that identifies the provision that a learner should receive to support their needs.

IGGY – International Gateway for Gifted Youth. The programme based at Warwick University which provided an online community for HLP young people.

Local offer – what is provided in a local area to support SEND.

MAT – multi-academy trust. Type of school.

MSI – multisensory impairment. Combined hearing and visual impairment often with additional physical, sensory, medical or learning difficulties.

Neurodiversity – the range of differences in individual brain function and behaviour traits regarded as part of the normal variation in the human population. Usually applied to things like Autism Spectrum Condition (ASC), HLP, DME.

NQT – newly qualified teacher.

RQT – recently qualified teacher.

SEN/SEND – when a person has one or more Special Educational Needs or Disabilities.

SENCO – Special Educational Needs Co-ordinator. The person responsible for co-ordinating Special Educational Needs (SEN) and/or Disabilities (SEND) work in a school.

VI – Visual impairment.

Appendix 2

DME support available for schools

There are many organisations both in the UK and overseas which support children with DME directly and no doubt a number of them have been inadvertently omitted from the lists below, for which apologies are given. Notwithstanding, by featuring these organisations, the authors make no comment on the quality of service offered or provided.

However, we hope that this information will provide a useful starting point to help schools to begin to build up their resources on DME and DME-related issues.

Key organisations in the UK supporting schools with DME issues

These are organisations who have specifically said that they have services of relevance to DME and have agreed to appear in this publication. This section provides their own words on what they do.

Table 6.1

Name	The Brilliant Club
Brief description	The Brilliant Club is a national university access charity that exists to increase the number of pupils from under-represented backgrounds progressing to highly-selective universities. It does this by mobilising the PhD community to share its academic expertise with state schools – either as part-time tutors or full-time classroom teachers.
	Through The Brilliant Club's award-winning Scholars Programme, small groups of pupils are supported by a PhD-level tutor over the course of a term to complete a university-style module culminating in a final assignment. These in-school tutorials are complemented by two trips to highly-selective universities.
	The programme is available for pupils aged 10-17 in any non-selective state school that wishes to participate. Last year the programme worked with over 700 schools and 13,000 pupils in every nation and region of the UK.
Services relevant to DME	Each term that schools sign up to The Scholars Programme they select a group of pupils to take part (minimum 12 pupils – two tutorial groups of six). It is up to schools to decide which pupils they feel will most benefit from the programme.
	The Brilliant Club works closely with schools to make sure that The Scholars Programme is accessible to all pupils they select, regardless of any additional needs they may have.
Tel	0207 939 1946
Email	hello@thebrilliantclub.org
Website	www.thebrilliantclub.org
Facebook	www.facebook.com/TheBrilliantClub
Twitter	@BrilliantClub
LinkedIn	www.linkedin.com/company/the-brilliant-club

Table 6.2

Name	British Mensa
Brief description	Mensa is primarily a social organisation for individuals whose IQ falls within the top 2% of the population. Our membership includes pre-schoolers, right through to those for whom work is just a distant memory. Most events are member-led and family members are welcome whether or not they have joined. There are face to face meetings, special interest groups, our monthly magazine, expert lectures, regional and national gatherings and much more.
	In terms of children and young people, we have a Family Mensa Facebook group which runs events all over the country and a Parent Support Group also on Facebook.
	Lyn Kendall is our Gifted Child Consultant and she runs seminars, lectures and workshops for adults as well as workshops for the children themselves. Each year we hold the 'Future Paths' conference at Oxford or Cambridge University for youngsters who set their sights high. There is an active mentoring programme in place. Mensa is a meeting of like minds and can be as much or as little as you want it to be.
	Lyn Kendall, our Gifted Child Consultant, is a psychologist and teacher with over 40 years' experience of working with children at both ends of the ability scale. She visits and advises schools and offers teacher training, advice on Access Arrangements as well as other services.
	Mensa can arrange group testing sessions in schools and support those establishments that are aiming to be a Mensa Hub School.
Services relevant to DME	Mensa is open to all individuals whose IQ falls within the top 2% of the population. We currently have members who have diagnoses of dyslexia, Autistic Spectrum Disorder, ADHD and so on. Lyn Kendall is happy to advise and support parents of children with DME.
Tel	01902 772 771
Email	Services@mensa.org.uk
Website	www.mensa.org.uk
Facebook	@BritishMensa
Twitter	@BritishMensa
Instagram	@britishmensa

Table 6.3

Name	Exscitec Ltd
Brief description	Exscitec was established as a private limited company in 2000. Its prime function is to provide STEM education support to a variety of clients.
	Exscitec has worked with university clients in terms of widening access initiatives and has also supported specific groups through the provision of STEM activities, including organisations that work with children with DME and groups of looked after children, some of whom fall on the Autistic Spectrum.
	More recently our work has included consultancy to the Ministry and some Departments of Education in Vietnam.
Services relevant to DME	Bespoke design and delivery of STEM activities and programmes for DME students of all ages.
	Programme management of STEM activities and programmes for educational and commercial sectors including bursary programmes, national challenges and STEM Award schemes.
	Management and delivery of non-residential and residential courses.
	Recruitment and pastoral support for educational events and programmes.
	Exscitec programmes such as Summer Camps provide a secure mentor supported non-school based environment within which students can explore and engage STEM activities.
Tel	**(+44)1730 261 458**
Email	**info@exscitec.com**
Website	www.exscitec.com
Twitter	**@alanwest15**

Table 6.4

Name	GIFT
Brief description	GIFT has been providing opportunities for HLP and DME youngsters to meet one another and learn for over 40 years. What began as a group of specialist teachers within Essex county council has continued as a private organisation that runs residential and day courses and online seminars embracing everything from philosophy to rocketry to improvisation. The informality, small groups and cherishing of individual differences make GIFT a place where children with HLP or DME can find their tribe and thrive intellectually and socially, with many making life-long friendships.
	GIFT is generously supported by charities and ex-GIFTers, so that bursaries are often available. We have always managed to enable those who want to attend our courses to do so.
Services relevant to DME	Residential Easter, Summer and weekend courses for secondary age students. Monthly online philosophy seminars. Advice for schools and advocacy for parents.
Tel	**01245 830321**
Email	**enquiries@giftcourses.co.uk**
Website	www.giftcourses.co.uk
Facebook	**fb.me/giftcourses**
Twitter	**@giftcourses**

Table 6.5

Name	National Association for Able Children in Education (NACE)
Brief description	An independent charity, NACE works with schools, education leaders, practitioners and policy makers to improve provision for more able learners, driving whole-school improvement and raising standards in provision for all. Drawing on over 35 years' experience in the field, we offer support across all sectors, phases, contexts and stages of development.
	United by a shared focus on improving provision for more able learners and promoting challenge for all, our members have access to regularly updated guidance, CPD, peer exchange, school-led research initiatives, and the opportunity to join the NACE Challenge Development Programme – supporting ongoing whole-school review and improvement.
	Annual NACE membership gives your school the chance to be part of an established learning community – dedicated to driving forward and disseminating effective provision for the more able.
	Membership covers all staff in a school, offering year-round support and guidance both online and in person.
Services relevant to DME	The NACE Challenge Development Programme is designed to support school leaders who are uncompromising in their ambition to ensure all more able learners achieve their potential, in the context of challenge for all. The programme is founded on the NACE Challenge Framework, a well-established tool for whole-school review and improvement, with accompanying resources, consultancy, CPD and opportunities for school-to-school working.
	Comprehensive and robust in its criteria, the programme can be used by schools and groups of schools at all phases, sectors and contexts – including those already demonstrating good or outstanding provision for more able learners, as well as those for whom this is a key area for improvement. It is regularly reviewed to ensure it supports current areas of emphasis in school improvement and accountability, including expectations set out in the Ofsted, Estyn, ISI and other evaluation schedules.
Tel	**01235 425000**
Email	**info@nace.co.uk**
Website	www.nace.co.uk
Twitter	**@naceuk**

Table 6.6

Name	Nisai Group
Brief description	For over 22 years, we have delivered flexible, innovative education programmes to our learners and supported them to achieve their ambitions.
	At Nisai, we are much more than online learning. We provide a friendly, supportive learning community and offer our students incredible opportunities. In essence we support learners up to the age of 25 and help create pathways to further education and employment through personalised learning.
	We believe that everyone has equal value and should have access to high quality education around the world.
	We support learning barriers through innovative education that is accessible and affordable to all. We provide a holistic learning experience for both traditional and non-traditional learners.
Services relevant to DME	Many high achieving students struggle between their ability level and their age of maturity, which in mainstream schools can result in bullying and disengagement. At Nisai, we time-table our learners at their current working level rather than their age. This enables them to study alongside learners who may be older and at a higher maturity level than they are. Coupled with well-paced, interactive lessons, this creates the ideal working environment for HLP and DME learners.
	Our teaching staff are all subject specialists and have received supplementary training to support students with additional needs.
	Our dedicated Customer and Student Support Team can offer support outside the classroom for both parents and schools.
Tel	**+44 208 424 8475**
Email	**David.lester@nisai.com**
Website	www.nisai.com
Facebook	www.facebook.com/NisaiLearningPage/
Twitter	https://twitter.com/NisaiLearning
LinkedIn	www.linkedin.com/company/nisai

Table 6.7

Name	North West Gifted and Talented (known as NWGT)
Brief description	NWGT is a small regional charity whose role is to support schools throughout the North West in meeting the needs of their able, gifted and talented learners.
	Support for Teachers
	NWGT runs a range of regional CPD courses throughout each academic year. NWGT is also able to provide support for individual schools. This can range from whole school INSET days to working with individual A, G & T Leads on developing school practice. This area of work can also include advice and guidance in respect of individual learners.
	Activities for Pupils
	We organise and lead Saturday Challenges throughout the region. These enable young people to come together to explore areas of learning alongside an expert and in conjunction with other young people with similar interests. We offer a broad range of Challenges that enable learners to further develop skills and talents directly linked to the school curriculum and to explore areas beyond the curriculum.
	We also offer Challenge workshops during the school day. These can be off the shelf workshops from our *Challenge Brochure* or bespoke activities developed to meet the specific requirements of an individual school or group of schools.
	Masterclasses
	A recent initiative was the introduction of a series of master classes for exceptionally able primary mathematicians, writers and scientists from Y2 – Y6. These are held in partnership with local universities. These events also act as CPD for teachers as a group of children and a teacher attend together and work alongside each other. The teacher is then provided with all the activities to use back in school

Name	*North West Gifted and Talented (known as NWGT)*
Services relevant to DME	All our activities are inclusive and cater for DME. The director of NWGT also specialises in providing support to individual schools to ensure that they are able to meet the needs of children with DME.
Tel	07973 119653
Email	aileen.hoare@northwestgiftedandtalented.org.uk
Website	www.northwestgiftedandtalented.org.uk

Table 6.8

Name	*Potential Plus UK (formerly known as NAGC – The National Association for Gifted Children)*
Brief description	Potential Plus UK is an independent charity supporting young people with High Learning Potential, including those with dual or multiple exceptionalities, by working with families and schools. Our aim is that every High Learning Potential young person in England and Wales receives appropriate support and challenge to secure wellbeing and high attainment with the skills, resilience and confidence to succeed at each stage. Every year we support thousands of young people through building and sustaining communities of support, improving provision, raising awareness and supporting young people to develop self-understanding and leadership skills.
Services relevant to DME	Website information, advice service, advice sheets for families and schools, events for families, training for teachers and SENCOs.
Tel	01908 646433
Email	amazingchildren@potentialplusuk.org
Website	www.potentialplusuk.org
Facebook	PotentialPlusUk
Twitter	Twitter: @PPUK_
Instagram	potentialplusuk.uk

Table 6.9

Name	*(The) Potential Trust*
Brief description	The Potential Trust is an educational charity set up to provide, promote, and encourage whatever makes education more interesting and exciting for children of High Learning Potential (including children and young people with DME), especially events and experiences that facilitate the children's personal and social development, and their practical and artistic skills as well as their intellectual ones.
Services relevant to DME	The Trust helps to fund small conferences (up to about 20 people) for teachers and other professionals who want to discuss DME and DME-related issues. Funding will be provided for food and accommodation but not travel or other costs, The Trust will also consider supporting small-scale projects exclusively for children or young people with DME although there are guidelines for this.
Tel	01844 351666
Email	thepotentialtrust@clara.co.uk

Table 6.10

Name	*PowerWood, happily unique*
Brief description	PowerWood offers advocacy and support for professionals, families and individuals of all ages that work/live with specific traits. The traits are having a high ability or High Learning Potential combined with intensity, sensitivity, hyper-reactivity, learning difficulties, uneven development, emotion regulation (including being easily overwhelmed) or mental health issues.
	This combination is called Dual and Multiple Exceptionality (DME – in the UK) or Twice Exceptionality (2e – in the US).
	Individuals with neurodiversity (including DME and 2e) are often misunderstood, sometimes even misdiagnosed. They might be seen as lazy, unwilling or unintelligent.
	PowerWood celebrates, cherishes and embraces Neurodiversity as a natural variation, a personal strength and a positive asset to our community.
	A typical neurodiverse bright child/teen/young person's emotional reactions might be a barrier to their achievements and can be challenging to support. To improve families and individuals' quality of life, PowerWood offers information, strategies, tools and theories that are cutting-edge research-based. We develop, trial, test strategies that are tailored to personal choices, beliefs and circumstances, based on the parents' experience and feedback.
	PowerWood's support for professionals*, enables them to help single and groups neurodiverse individuals to use their strengths, energy and abilities towards self-appreciation and harmonious family life, emotion regulation, empowering an individual to pursue their self-chosen goals, passions and dreams.
	*All services to professionals are delivered by Simone de Hoogh, founding director of PowerWood and ECHA Specialist in Gifted Education, fields of expertise: High-Ability, DME/2e, Neurodiversity, Emotion Regulation, Compassionate Effective Communication and Narrowing Behaviour (behaviours traditionally associated with mental health issues).
Services relevant to DME	**PowerWood for Professionals**
	PowerWood offers tailored **Workshops** for schools* tackling various subjects linked with Neurodiversity.
	PowerWood offers tailored **educational consultancy sessions*** for educational and health care professionals surrounding a specific neurodiverse child with several diagnoses for whom an adapted educational plan has to be developed.
	PowerWood offers **individual online support sessions** to children and teens to help them develop self-appreciation, emotion regulation and executive functioning skills, with an aim to enhance their general experience of life and learning.
	For more information, please email and you will be invited to a Free Introductory Talk online to discuss possible options in your specific situation.
Tel	**Office T. +44 (0) 20 329 05 764 Monday – Friday 9-11am during term time (UK landline)**
Email	office@powerwood.org.uk
Website	www.powerwood.org.uk/
Facebook	www.facebook.com/PowerWoodUK
Closed Facebook Group	PowerWood offers a closed moderated friendly FaceBook Group where people can meet others facing the same challenges and support each www.facebook.com/groups/1648425685414993/
Twitter	https://twitter.com/PowerWoodUK
Instagram	www.instagram.com/powerwood.neurodiversity/
LinkedIn	www.linkedin.com/in/simonepowerwood
YouTube	www.youtube.com/channel/UCY4TG2kEimJ5SgJbdT0QzRQ
Pinterest	https://pinterest,.co.uk/PowerWoodUK/
Newsletter	http://eepurl.combJq5iX

Table 6.11

Name	*SNAP (Scottish Network for Able Pupils)*
Brief description	The Scottish Network for Able Pupils has specialised in teaching and learning for highly able pupils for over 20 years. SNAP has offered support and advice to the Scottish Education system in three main areas: publications, staff development and national conferences. Working in the field of both Special Educational Needs/Additional Support Needs and Gifted and Talented Education, SNAP have an interest in, and considerable experience of, working with teachers as they support children of high ability
	SNAP also offers opportunities to study at master's level through the Masters in Inclusive Education: research, policy and practice at the University of Glasgow. Courses are available through distance learning as well as face to face and twilight classes.
Services relevant to DME	*Offering a network of support to schools and teachers through sharing ideas and practise;
	*Providing forums for debate and discussion;
	*Offering advice to schools and teachers on how to provide appropriate challenge for their most able children;
	*Providing the educational community in Scotland with opportunities to hear and question international leaders in the field of 'gifted and talented' education;
	*Undertaking research and disseminating the findings to the educational community in Scotland and further afield;
	*Acting as a critical friend for school-based innovation and offering advice and information to policy makers.
Tel	**+44 141 330 3072**
Email	**education-SNAP@glasgow.ac.uk**
Website	www.ablepupils.com
Facebook	www.facebook.com/groups/1440065662944724/?ref=bookmarks
Twitter	@tanzania8 @Eavanmac

Table 6.12

Name	*Tomorrow's Achievers*
Brief description	Provides specialist masterclasses for exceptionally able children around the UK
Services relevant to DME	Children with DME are welcome to attend the Masterclasses.
Tel	020 3865 7170
Email	Patricia@coramtomorrowsachievers.org.uk
Website	www.tomorrowsachievers.co.uk
Facebook	@TomorrowsAchievers
Twitter	@Tom_Achievers

Table 6.13

Name	*Villiers Park Educational Trust*
Brief description	Villiers Park Educational Trust is a national social mobility charity working with high ability 14-18 year olds from less advantaged backgrounds. We provide a number of different educational programmes which help young people achieve their potential. Our students say the charity's intervention inspires them to aim for better universities and more ambitious career choices, through increased self-confidence and a determination to do as well as, if not better than, their more affluent peers.

(Continued)

Table 6.13 (Contd.)

Name	*Villiers Park Educational Trust*
Services relevant to DME	Our educational offer includes the Inspiring Excellence Programme which is made up of university standard, subject specific, courses, both STEM and the arts. Students enjoy full board and lodgings at our headquarters in Foxton, Cambridgeshire, during their course. Many students say the IEP has helped them with future decisions about university and career choices, as well as putting them in touch with like-minded young people. While Villiers Park Educational Trust does not provide specific support for DME or SEND students, we welcome all high ability young people from a state-educated background.
Tel	01223 872601
Email	VP@villierspark.org.uk
Website	www.villierspark.org.uk
Facebook	@VilliersPark
Twitter	@VilliersPark
Instagram	villierspark
YouTube	VilliersPark

Interesting books on DME

Table 6.14

	Title	*Author*	*Publisher*	*Year of Publication*
1.	*Gifted and Talented Children with Special Education Needs: Double Exceptionality*	Diane Montgomery	Nace/Fulton	2003
2.	*Teaching Gifted Children with Special Educational Needs*	Diane Montgomery	Routledge	2015
3.	*Misdiagnosis and Dual Diagnoses of Gifted Children and Adults*	F. Richard Olenchak, Jean Goerss, Paul Belzan, James T Webb, Nadia E. Webb and Edward R. Amend	Great Potential Press	2005
4.	*To Be Gifted and Learning Disabled: Strengths-Based Strategies for Helping 2e Students*	Susan Baum, Steven Owen and Robin Schader	Prufock Press	2017
5.	*Gifted Lives*	Joan Freeman		2010
6.	*Twice Exceptional: Supporting and Educating Bright and Creative Students with Learning Difficulties*	Scott Barry Kaufman	Oxford University Press	2018
7.	*Effective Provision for Able and Exceptionally Able Children*	Valsa Koshy and Ron Casey	Hodder Education	1997
8.	*Living with Intensity: Understanding the Sensitivity, Excitability and Emotional Development of Gifted Children, Adolescents and Adults*	Susan Daniels and Michael Piechowski	Great Potential Press	2009
9.	*Giftedness 101*	Linda Silverman	Springer Publishing	2013
10.	*Am I Autistic?*	Lydia Andal	New Idealist	2015

Links to some useful organisations overseas relevant for DME

Most of the organisations featured below are primarily about HLP rather than DME. This is often the starting point for research about DME. They have been chosen because they have DME-related elements on their website which may be relevant for schools.

Table 6.15

American Association for Gifted Children https://aagc.ssri.duke.edu	**ECHA** **(European Council for High Ability)** www.echa.info	**National Association for Gifted Children (US)** www.nagc.org/
The Association for Bright Children of Ontario www.abcontario.ca/	**Gifted and Talented Children's Association of South Australia** http://gtcasa.asn.au/about/	**New Zealand Association for Gifted Children (nzagc)** www.giftedchildren.org.nz/
Australian Association for the Education of the Gifted and Talented www.aaegt.net.au/	**Gifted Development Center** www.gifteddevelopment.com	**Queensland Association for Gifted and Talented Children** www.qagtc.org.au
Australian Gifted Student Support Centre https://australiangiftedsupport.com	**GERRIC (Gifted Education Research Resource and Information Centre** https://education.arts.unsw.edu.au/about-us/gerric/	**SENG (Supporting Emotional Needs of the Gifted** www.sengifted.org/about
Center for Talent Development www.ctd.northwestern.edu/aboutctd	**Gifted and Talented Ireland** http://giftedandtalented.ie/	**Tasmanian Association for the Gifted Inc** www.tasgifted.com/
Council for Exceptional Children www.cec.sped.org/	**Hong Kong Academy for Gifted Education** www.hkage.org.hk	**Victorian Association for Gifted and Talented Children** www.vagtc.org.au
Davidson Institute for Talent Development www.davidsongifted.org	**John Hopkins Center for Talented Youth** https://cty.jhu.edu	**World Council for Gifted and Talented Children** https://world-gifted.org

Other useful resources specific to DME

Table 6.16

Dr Devon's Blog	https://drdevon.com/category/blog/	Articles on 2e DME and gifted learners by psychologist Dr Devon Maceachron
Gifted and Talented International	www.tandfonline.com/toc/ugti20/current	Journal from the World Council on gifted and talented children. Includes articles about DME issues
Gifted Child Today	https://journals.sagepub.com/description/gct	Resources on a range of issues including DME
Gifted Issues: 2e Forum	http://giftedissues.davidsongifted.org/BB/ubbthreads.php/topics/36244/2e_Twice_Exceptional_Newslette.html#Post36244	Blog posts on 2e from the Davidson Institute

(Continued)

Table 6.16 (Contd.)

'Good Career Guidance: Perspectives from the Special Educational Needs and Disabilities Sector'	www.goodcareerguidance.org.uk/assets/file?filePath=send/good-career-guidance-perspectives-from-the-send-sector.pdf	UK publication produced in July 2019 by Gatsby, Careers Enterprise Company and Disability Rights UK and mentions DME
GT World	http://gtworld.org/links.html	Links to useful resources
Educational Resources Information Center on Disabilities and Gifted Education	www.washington.edu/doit/educational-resources-information-center-eric-clearinghouse-disabilities-and-gifted-education	This US organisation gathers and disseminates professional literature, information and resources on the education and development of individuals of all ages who have disabilities and/or who are gifted
2e: Twice Exceptional	http://2emovie.com/	Films about 2e by Thomas Ropelewski including one about Teaching the 2e
2e Newsletter	www.2enewsletter.com	For parents, educators and other professionals helping children reach their potential
Hoagies	www.hoagiesgifted.org/what_is_2e.htm	Resources on 2e
Mind Matters Pod	@MindMattersPod	Mind Matters podcast which features conversations with the best minds in psychology, education and a variety of issues including 2e (DME)
Tilt Parenting	@TiltParenting	Top podcast and community for parents with 'differently wired' children (including ADHD, 2e, ASD, gifted, anxious and learning difficulties). May be of some interest to teachers and other professionals in schools.
Understood	www.understood.org/en	Formed when 15 non-profit organisations joined forces to support parents with children with learning difficulties and attention issues including DME. Has a blog
Uniquely Gifted	www.uniquelygifted.org	A range of resources to support gifted children with Special Educational Needs (children and young people with DME)

Useful Twitter handles

Table 6.17

TWITTER	
@AboveBeyondAwards	Twitter link to Above and Beyond Award. Awards in the UK for schools and others including DME work.
@CECTAG	TAG embraces and supports the needs of students with gifts and talents, focusing on 2e and other diverse learners through advocacy, professional learning and resources.
@drdanpeters	Dr Dan Peters is a psychologist at the Summit Centre and an author of books on creativity, anxiety and gifted and 2e issues.

TWITTER	
@GiftedEdIa	Tweets about gifted and talented, profoundly gifted, gifted education and 2e. Resources for parents, educators and policymakers.
@hellototko	TOTKO is the UK's first organisation to provide workshops, peer support and information on all learning differences.
@ncldorg	National Centre for Learning Disabilities.
@Oregon2e	Everything about 2e from Oregon in the USA.
@senmagazine	UK magazine. Have run articles on DME.
@2ENews	Twice Exceptional consulting and mentoring in Chicago and with national reach via the Gifted Parents website www.giftedparents.org.
@2enewsdotcom	Promotes understanding of Twice Exceptional education and neurodiversity.
@2xceptional	Empowering kids and adults to overcome learning challenges and to make a difference in the world. www.2xceptional.com.
@Teca2e	Twice Exceptional Children's Advocacy (TECA) was formed in 2003 by a group of parents seeking to identify, support and unite 2e students and their families.
@2eDansk	Twice Exceptional Denmark. Information from Denmark about DME.

Appendix 3

Ten myths of supporting pupils with DME

Myth No. 1: You cannot have a Special Educational Need or Disability and be highly able at the same time.

Myth No. 2: Having HLP makes up for having a Special Educational Need or Disability.

Myth No. 3: Pupils cannot have HLP and lack basic skills; it just means they are lazy or aren't trying.

Myth No. 4: How can more able pupils struggle so much with their working memory or processing speed; are they just not listening?

Myth No. 5: Abilities and Special Educational Needs cannot be addressed at the same time.

Myth No. 6: Pupils with DME cannot go onto our school's HLP programme, they would slow down the other pupils.

Myth No. 7: Addressing the pupil's weaknesses must be the top priority for our pupils with DME.

Myth No. 8: Pupils with DME should be more mature than other pupils their own age.

Myth No. 9: Pupils with DME can't have EHC plans or IEPs or the equivalent.

Myth No. 10: It would require too many resources to provide for learners with DME at the same time as everyone else.

Index

Note: References in *italics* are to figures, those in **bold** to tables.